The Second Seasonal Political Palate

A FEMINIST VEGETARIAN COOKBOOK

BY THE BLOODROOT COLLECTIVE
BETSEY BEAVEN
NOEL FURIE
SELMA MIRIAM

DESIGN AND PRODUCTION BY BUFFY PARKER
PHOTOGRAPHY BY NOEL FURIE
COVER ILLUSTRATION BY LAURA LOUISE FOSTER

SANGUINARIA PUBLISHING
85 FERRIS STREET
BRIDGEPORT, CONNECTICUT 06605

We encourage the reproduction of up to five recipes and any of the introductory material, properly credited, for feminist and vegetarian purposes. Please write us for more information and/or recipe exchange.

©1984 Sanguinaria Publishing
85 Ferris Street, Bridgeport, CT 06605

10   9   8   7   6   5   4   3   2   1

ISBN 0-9605210-2-X

Library of Congress Catalog Card No. 84-052064

DEDICATION

For Alicia

Who understands the necessity
of a women's space,
Whose rage confirms ours,
Who has struggled with us over differences
in our mutual attempt to understand
issues between us and events in our movement.

We are grateful for her feminist vision,
her courage, and her loyalty.
She continues to renew our faith
in the possibilities ahead.

ACKNOWLEDGMENTS

Various parts of this book have benefited from the assistance of
Adelita Chirino, Ann Alves, Batya Bauman, Betsy Gooch, Dennis
O'Neill, Donna Osborne, Elaine Ward, Gabriella Aynat, Krystina
Colburn, Marianne Nicolosi, Mary Ellen McCarthy, Mary McDonnell,
Pat Shea, Phyllis Chesler, Sandra Anderson, and Sarah Jaeger.

Bloodroot has been shaped by many besides ourselves. Most
important are those who do the day to day work necessary to keep
a women's place going. Part of our recent history were: Karen
Bernstein, Sharon Leslie, Dawn McDaniel, Jill Bomser, Sandy
Martin, Barbara Beckelman, Caroline Forbes, Judy Mortner, Susan
Smith, Robin Baslow, and Georgia Merola. Currently Betsy
Gooch continues with us; as do Marie Gall, with her instinct for
friendship and the way she has made it a bridge; Meg Profetto,
whose cheerful spirit has helped more often than she knows; and
Elaine Ward, who has become rooted with us, to our great pleasure.

We thank Maris Hearne, for her gift of typesetting; Jonathan Cappel
particularly for his efforts this year; and Adelita Chirino, for the
quality of her loyalty.

We are here at Bloodroot because we want to make a women's
space. Those who come to partake of the food, the books, and the
conversation mean more to us than they may realize, whether they
come often or only once.

This past year, a difficult one, had moments of special joy. In
particular, to celebrate our bookstore expansion, Barbara Smith,
Alma Gómez, Michelle Cliff, and Susan Yung (Kitchen Table Press)
came to speak one very rainy night. Adrienne Rich shared her
warmth with us. Audre Lorde's visit cleansed, healed, and fired us.
Chrystos and Beth Brant lit up our mermaid room with their words
on a stormy night. Others who brightened a dark time with their
respective visits include Sudie Rakusin and her paintings, Beth
Karbe, Laura Wetzler and her singing, Sonia Johnson, Myriam
Foujere, Louise, Martine Giguere, Batya Bauman, and Mary Daly,
who by inspiring us to remember our vision and to live our dreams,
encourages our persistence.

And finally, Donna Osborne and Sandra Anderson continue to
make themselves a constant resource for us. They are, in the best
meaning of the word, family.

TABLE OF CONTENTS

INTRODUCTION

In 1980, we wrote and published *The Political Palate,* a feminist vegetarian cookbook based on the seasonal recipes we serve in our restaurant. This, *The Second Seasonal Political Palate* is a companion volume. Both books are more than collections of recipes. They document our interest in ethnic and ethical cooking, our commitment to feminism, our growth as individual women living and working collectively. This volume, then, illustrates the changes that have occurred in the last four years.

I. CHANGES IN MENU

Once *The Political Palate* had gone to the printer and the months of reducing quantities in recipes, trying to write clearly, endless editing and proofreading were over, there were suddenly a number of new dishes to try. We also decided to stop serving fish altogether: there was plenty of good food on the menu without it, and by then we had a clientele who seemed willing to try new dishes. Those who wanted fish would have to go elsewhere. Friends brought us new recipes, and we continued to experiment with tofu, miso, tempeh, and the various grains. Since we still use virtually all the recipes in *The Political Palate,* there is hardly time to serve all the dishes we and our customers like so much. We continue to cook as much as we can according to the seasons, choosing what we make by what is best in market or garden.

In the last four years a few inspirational vegetarian cookbooks have appeared. We are particularly excited by *World of the East Vegetarian Cooking* by Maddhur Jaffrey, *Classic Armenian Recipes: Cooking Without Meat* by Antreassian and Jebejian and some of the new Crossing Press titles such as *Elegant Eating for Hard Times* and *The Spice Box.* Earlier books, (with a few exceptions such as Julie Jordan's *Wings of Life,)* were often disappointing to us as serious vegetarian cooks. Also there seems to be a growing public consciousness that vegetarianism is healthier than meat eating. Citing a number of studies, health reporter Jane E. Brody noted that vegetarians, even dairy consuming ones, had lower cholesterol levels, lower blood pressure, and less cancer. Additionally, in regard to cancer, ". . . there is evidence that protective factors in vegetables, beans and whole grains may also be involved."[1]

While we consider this health-centered orientation problematic (as will be discussed later), it does mean that today a vegetarian is likely to find ideas and foods more readily available and is more likely to be taken seriously.[2]

[1] From an article originally printed in *The New York Times,* reprinted in *Vegetarian Times,* May, 1984.

[2] To explore the differences between our biology and that of true carnivores, see *What's Wrong With Eating Meat?* by Barbara Parham. This brief and inexpensive book explains arguments for vegetarianism in a gentle but convincing manner.

II. FEMINISM IN THE EIGHTIES

Feminism proceeds into the eighties as nuclear
proliferation grows, acid rain and general pollution
worsen, and the escalation of everyday violence against
women and children continues. Everyone we know is
frantically trying to see Reagan defeated. Discouragement
is rife, and yet there always seems to be hope. Why else
would Sonia Johnson run for President? In *Womanspirit*,
Summer 1984, Johnson wrote:

> So where can we turn for hope? Being revolutionaries, which we
> are, means that we're distinguished from the rest of the
> population by the fact that we have hope. The world, and the
> Women's Movement right now, is characterized by a very deep
> despair. We're the ones who are not despairing, and who
> understand that if we despair, all is lost. There always has to be
> not just hope, but real honest-to-goodness faith and trust in
> ourselves, in one another and our ability to make the new world
> and to make it happen in our lifetime.
>
> Because, another assumption that the System always teaches
> people is that you can work and work, and maybe some day you
> can change it. But it won't be in *your* lifetime. Maybe your
> children will see it.
>
> Well, who said we couldn't make a difference in our lifetime? It
> was Them. It was the enemy. Of course we can make a difference!
> And we must. Because if we don't do it in our lifetime, there won't
> be any more lifetime for anybody.

We are surprised at the growth in feminist
consciousness in many circles, even while we are
dismayed at the backlash and at the number of women
who give up under the pressures of phallocracy.

When we began Bloodroot in 1977, we were encouraged
by the growing women's movement and believed we
would be one of many working in that community.
We've since discovered that many feminist-oriented
businesses started in that year, and many of those are
gone now, though new ventures start all the time. There
is a difference between community and movement.

Oppressed communities often find themselves bonding in weakness. A feminist *movement,* on the other hand, requires vision and persistence as well as a recognition of the ways patriarchy can divide us. Struggling to remove the embedded self-hate and fragmentation of patriarchy is very difficult indeed. We are more affected by the reactionary politics of the eighties than most of us realize. As the struggle gets harder, success seems that much further off and many women feel "burnt out".

The media has exclaimed that here we are in 1984 and it's not as bad as predicted. It seems worse to us in many ways. What we see, concomitant with growing political conservatism, is encouragement for women to return to make-up and high heels and a romanticizing of childbirth. We see that *The New York Times Magazine* has joined the growing ranks of soft-porn periodicals, and domestic and sexual violence have increased sharply, not only in severity but in propensity. Aren't more and more women suffering from breast and uterine problems unheard of years ago? The forests and lakes are dying. The United States military industrial complex is encouraging the destruction of third-world natural resources, and worse, their patterns of survival. A litany of disasters.

Meanwhile here at home, computer literacy is touted as a necessary tool for feminist endeavors. We seem to be unable to learn that technology *per se* is not politically neutral, that the kind of knowledge we need is neither of better bombs nor of better software, that even disregarding physical damage done to women (especially third world) who make or work on computer machinery, communication by machine is not the answer. It is a giant step in the separation of our lives from real experience. As André Collard has written in *Trivia #2:* "Disconnecting Mother Earth from what she

brings forth is a tradition deeply entrenched in the Western mind. It is most noticeable among the scientific brotherhood, where the reductionistic, mechanistic approach to nature conceals the inability to respond to life with aesthetic emotion. When applied to language, this approach yields a mathematical science based on the mechanics of transmitting information for manipulative purposes rather than on the very real art of communicating experience. Not surprisingly, computer 'language' derives from such studies."

It is important to remember, as we use our electric lights, drive our cars, or consider word processors that it is not merely the motives of those employing technology which are at issue. We believe feminist goals must be to reconnect with living creatures and the earth, to try to lead self-sustaining lives with some understanding of the lives of other humans, creatures, and of the earth. We must question just what is appropriate technology, while we recognize the damage computer thinking is doing and will increasingly do to our lives. Chrystos, a Native American woman, writing about our participation in technology in *This Bridge Called My Back* asks: "Who is not guilty of being a thief? Who among us gives back as much as we take? Who among us has enough respect? Does anyone know the proper proportions?"

III. ETHICAL VEGETARIANISM

It is important to explain once again why we, as feminsts, are ethical vegetarians[3]. It is amazing to us that so many human animals don't want to know that other thinking and feeling creatures (the overwhelming majority of them female[4]) are tortured and killed so that we may eat meat or consume "safely" tested drugs and cosmetics. As Carol Adams writes: "Feminists explain sexism through animal metaphors, while unquestioningly accepting the speciesism which permits animal abuse. The implication is that how we treat other animals is lamentable if they were anything but non-human animals. We should remember that while women may *feel* like a piece of meat, and *be treated* like pieces of meat, animals *are* pieces of meat."[5]

Adams conceptualizes human stages of eating as fourfold: The first is characterized by reliance on plant foods in societies where the first tools enabled women

---

[3] Other connections between animal oppression and sexism have been explored brilliantly by Aviva Cantor in "The Club, the Yoke, and the Leash", *Ms. Magazine,* August 1983:

"Nowhere is patriarchy's iron fist as naked as in the oppression of animals, which serves as the model and training ground for all other forms of oppression.

"Its three basic strategies — the club, the yoke, and the leash — operate similarly in the oppression of women and minorities. The club strategy is to kill animals for gain, sadistic pleasure, and the 'affirmation of manhood'. It is domination through brute force. The yoke strategy is to domesticate animals to carry burdens and pull vehicles; supply eggs, wool, and milk; and provide flesh and skins. It is domination through enslavement. The leash strategy is to tame animals to provide the psychic benefits of direct rule of master over pet. It is domination through deceit."

[4] If we consider the *number* of individual animals eaten, they are overwhelmingly female (poultry). On a pound for pound basis, males (as beef) are probably eaten in comparable amounts. From conversations with Carol Adams and Jim Mason.

[5] Carol Adams, *The Edible Complex*, awaiting publication.

to collect plant proteins to bring back to children and community. The second stage was predominantly vegetarian with some reliance on hunting, typified by Native Americans. Third stage eating used domesticated animals together with plant proteins and centered on dairy production. (The racism of imposing dairy dependency on various peoples of color who can't tolerate milk products as happened in North America should be obvious. Continents such as Africa and North America before both were taken over by Europeans used no dairy products, and lactose intolerance is more widespread than is realized. Humans are the only mammals to use milk after infancy.) Finally, it is only since World War II that we have entered fourth stage eating — with animals institutionalized in factory farms. (For those who need information on the nature and growth of this "farming" see *Animal Factories* by Jim Mason and Peter Singer.) Besides the reality of this unspeakable cruelty to non-human animals, it is important to recognize that fourth stage eating cannot support itself. The quantity of "animalized"[6] protein assumed necessary for most typical USA diets oppresses and exploits the rest of the world. Note that 7% of the world's population (USA) consumes 30% of the world's animalized protein. Since it takes 17 to 20 pounds of grain or soy beans to produce one pound of edible beef, we are greedy consumers indeed.

Feminist vegetarians, reading mythographers like Joseph Campbell, can see that meat-eating cultures idealize ferocity, the territorial imperative, vitality and virility — what Carol Adams calls "The Blood Culture." Plant-based societies, on the other hand, celebrate a model of the wonder of life — in its cycle of growth and

---

[6] Carol Adams uses this word to clarify the fact that plants provide us with all we need in the way of protein. When we eat meat, the vegetables we need for survival have been "animalized."

decay, blossom and seed, wherein death and life appear as transformations of a single superordinated, indestructible force. In other words, harvest rather than violence, harmony with slow change of seasons rather than territoriality.

Myths/beliefs of the 80's are extremely health oriented. Almost every magazine cover promotes the current model of muscular anorexia. In the past eight years, Bloodroot customer concern has passed from issues such as why isn't all our flour whole wheat to why don't we have wheatless bread. *The Political Palate* was criticized for our use of cream and eggs, not because this use exploits animals, but because it is considered unhealthy to eat such fattening foods. At first sugar was evil, now all sweetening is. A few years ago, an extraordinary number of customers worried about mucous-producing foods and suffered from hypoglycemia. Most recently, wheat, corn, and fermentation allergies are surprisingly widespread. The newest "diseases" are eating disorders and ads offering help for these almost overshadow recent ones for stress management. Focus on stress itself by an affluent and privileged community is shocking. Stress has been said to "cause" or (in conjunction with drugs, pollution, junk food, sedentary life style, etc.) is "related to" cancer and other mysterious diseases. As a result health-oriented Americans have become obsessed with meditation, jogging, and stringent diets. No one seems to ask about stress suffered by poverty and starvation, by rape, by torture and murder, by the death of one's children, by twelve hours a day working on computer chips. "Stress Management" is a luxury of the privileged.

We remember when troubles were taken to priests, ministers and rabbis. Then troubles were taken to doctors and psychotherapists. These days nutritionists are thought to have the answers. To gain perspective on the latest fads in health, reread *For Her Own Good*, (Ehrenreich and English), the appropriate chapter on therapy in Mary Daly's *Gyn/Ecology*, (especially pages 282-285), and Jan Raymond's reflections in *The Transsexual Empire*. While we want to be generous hearted toward those with particular allergies, we are suspicious when there is an air of moral righteousness connected to the new diets. For ourselves, we assume that foods people have eaten for many centuries are likely to continue to be nutritious and that foods lower down on the food chain are less likely to contain concentrations of pollutants.[7] The history of the use of grains, fermented foods and oils is very ancient. What is new is our exceptional dependence on animalized proteins and fats.

Our vegetarianism stems from a broader base of reasoning than that of personal health. It comes from a foundation of thought based on feminist ethics: a consciousness of our connections with other species and with the survival of the earth. Of course we know that a diet based on grains and legumes, vegetables and

---

[7] While we recognize that agribusiness has poisoned the earth and polluted the waters, because meat represents a concentration of these same pollutants, we're still "better off" eating grains and legumes. Political action directed toward fighting agribusiness would be healthier than grain restricted diets.

fruits is personally healthy. But regardless of how much is learned about food combining, vitamins, basic food group needs, or about problems with pollution or chemical additives to meat, the fact remains that dependence on a meat and poultry diet is cruel and destructive to creatures more like ourselves than we are willing to admit — whether we mean turkeys and cows or the humans starved by land wasted for animal farming purposes to feed the privileged few. This is underscored by Martha M., in a letter to *Lesbian Contradiction,* Issue #6, Spring 1984:

> Even meat-eaters who believe any atrocity is justified if the victim is non-human and the beneficiary is human may want to consider the effects their dietary choices have on other humans and on themselves. We are all dependent, after all, on the rain forests of Central and South America ("the lungs of the world") for the maintenance of the world's ecological balance. And, as Catherine Caufield tells us, "since 1960 more than three quarters of all Central American forests have been destroyed to produce beef, most of which (more than 90%) is exported to the United States." Moreover, "the people who suffer most directly from the conversion of forest to pasture are the Indians who have lived in the forest for hundreds of years." And, "within a very few years of making the (Indians') land uninhabitable and forcing them to move elsewhere, the ranchers themselves will be forced to move on because their cattle will have exhausted the land."
>
> The same thing is happening in the Philippines. As Joan Gussow has written, "It must be emphasized here that we are no longer discussing a justice issue. We have gone beyond the question of whether it is fair for (the food I choose to eat) to be produced at the expense of some poor farmer's survival. It is my survival that is at stake. For what we are discussing here is the continued functioning on a world-wide scale of the system that provides the world with its food. Short of atomic war . . . there is probably no more serious problem that confronts us than the destruction produced by our business-as-usual assaults on the biosystem which sustains us all."

The point is, the devastating effects factory farming has on this earth are not mere coincidence, not simply by-products of a basically OK system. The devastation is a direct and inevitable result of our own attitudes and our own choices. As long as we treat the earth and its creatures as non-spiritual "resources" which exist only — or even primarily — for our benefit, we will continue to tear the world down around us.[8]

Unless we can learn that the value system inherent in our meat-eating patterns is one of brutality to human, food animals, and wild animals whose habitats are being destroyed, nothing we do for personal health reasons is truly healthy in the end. "For once stripped of their fundamental underpinnings, health issues may become reduced to narcissistic obsessions." (Carol Adams, Chap. 5: Thinking with our Hearts).

[8] Commenting on the spiritual quality of meat eating, Martha M. writes further: It is deeply frustrating to me that so few people recognize the connection between the devastating effects of factory farming and the Euro-US culture's de-spiritualization of non-human animals. We accept factory farming, most of us without even thinking about it, because we don't feel any reverence for the lives of non-human animals. A whale or a seal may inspire our imagination or our sentiment. But a cow? Don't be ridiculous! The intensive exploitation of cows — and pigs, sheep, chickens, etc. — is perfectly OK, even though it involves treatment we would never ever allow to be inflicted on an animal we knew or "identified with." If it's a cow, we just don't want to know, don't want to even hear about it, because it's just so easy and convenient and comfortable to enjoy the by-products of methodical torture and slaughter. References: Catherine Caufield quoted from "Big Mac Devours the Amazon," *Food Monitor*, Sept./Oct. 1982; and Joan Gussow quoted from "Food: Wanting & Needing & Providing," *Food Monitor*, July/Aug. 1983.

Meanwhile there is a new category of diseases called eating disorders. While psychotherapists and nutritionists claim to treat them, as feminists we require a political and sociological analysis of their proliferation. First it is important to recognize that the mania with weight reduction and anorexia/bulimia are different points on the same continuum of hatred for women's bodies. Mary Daly writes, under the heading "The Shrinking of Female Being," in *Gyn/Ecology*:

> . . . So also is a woman preoccupied who obsessively examines herself in a mirror, seeing herself as a parcel of protuberances. She is looking through male lenses. Filled with inspired fixations, she checks to see if hair, eyebrows, lashes, lips, skin, breasts, buttocks, stomach, hips, legs, feet are "satisfactory.". . .
>
> Gynecological/therapeutic/cosmetic preoccupation conceals the patient's emptiness from her Self. It drives the splintered self further into the state of fixation upon the parts that have become symbols of her lost and prepossessed Self. Reduced to the state of an empty vessel/vassal, the victim focuses desperately upon physical symptoms, therapeutically misinterpreted memories, and "appearance," frantically consuming medication, counsel, cosmetics, and clothing to cloak and fill her expanding emptiness. As she is transformed into an insatiable consumer, her transcendence is consumed and she consumes herself.[9]

The multiplicity of diet programs, groups, and books, as well as the frightening increase of anorexia among young women is proof that women have internalized body self-hate.

As Kim Chernin points out in *The Obsession: Reflections on the Tyranny of Slenderness,* appropriate weight is a matter of the decade in which you live. She believes feminism has been accompanied, first in the twenties and then in the seventies, with a backlash of hatred for women of size; Marilyn Monroe would be today's fat woman. "The reason, I say, that 98 percent of women gain back the weight they have lost (in diet

[9] Mary Daly, *Gyn/Ecology*, pp. 232-233.

programs) is simple — the weight belongs to us by nature."[10] It would seem to follow that if we accept variation in height, skin color, ableism, we should be able to recognize fatness as one of many forms of femaleness. *Shadow On A Tightrope,* a superb collection of writings by fat women, demonstrates that we do not. Edited by Lisa Schoenfielder and Barb Weiser, this book is must reading for those who wish to pursue the connections between anorexia, dieting, and the oppression of fat women, and therefore to appreciate why we need fat politics to understand eating disorders. "Consider that control over our bodies is the bottom line of the women's movement" (by Marjory Nelson, "Fat and Old, Old and Fat"). And "Dieting is starvation, it is self-abuse, it is self-hate" (by Kelly, "Medical Crimes"). Other articles in this book which explore political aspects of negative attitudes on weight include "The Goddess is Fat", "Conversation With Nancy", "Some Thoughts On Fat", and the excellent forward.

The more we explore old cookbooks, recipes from other cultures, or ruminate on what folks ate 50 or 100 years ago the more apparent it becomes that grains have been the food base of most peoples: rice, wheat, corn, millet, rye, barley, etc. Grains were the staple harvested from the wild or from planted crops. Earliest women gathered grains and devised ways to carry them back for sharing or storing. Fruits and vegetables supplemented the grains. Fish were and are eaten by peoples near water and meat has been used as an occasional condiment. It is only in the post war years that meat has become an obsession in this country: a three-meal-a-day obsession that we are exporting as a value system to other countries, spreading starvation as

[10] Kim Chernin, *The Obsession,* p. 30.

a result. Grains have been associated with the earth's abundance or what patronizing writers call fertility goddesses.[11] Grains are our mothers. Demeter and wheat and the corn mother are but two examples. Our sustenance and life blood comes from grains. All over the earth, oldest images of both mother and food are personified in Goddesses of grains: Chicomecoatel, the Aztec Goddess of food symbolized by a double ear of corn; Ceres/Demeter, whose recurrent image is wheat or barley; Dewi Sri, the Javanese rice Goddess.[12] Ever since the precepts of psychotherapy have acquired general influence, women have been told our problems are because of our mothers. In the fifties, we were told we were neurotic because of them. Now the latest wrinkle is allergies to wheat, corn, and fermentation, continuing the tradition. We prefer to remember the value of grains, legumes ("that which is gathered"), fruits, whether fresh or fermented, yeasted, brewed, in all stages from seed to decay. These are what sustain us.

[11] MAIZE, MAIS, from the original Haitian: SUSTAINER OF LIFE. She is Blessed Daughter, Seed of Seeds, Sacred Mother among the indigenous peoples of the Western Hemisphere, and known by English-speaking North Americans, simply, as corn. Maize and life are one. The origin histories of Mayan descendants remind all people that our bodies were sculpted by the deities from the dough of ground maize. Growing of the crop and every mouthful of the grain continues the creation of the divine ones. Among the deities, the rites and cultivation of maize, womyn were essential. Among some North American nations, a womon would remove her clothes, alone, in the dark of the moon, to drag them around the newly planted field — a ritual to ensure safety and a plentiful harvest. A womon from the Iroquois, a nation in which womyn had much tribal power, stated, "You should understand that it is the women, not the men who have the function of producing life. If they do the planting, the cornstalk produces two or three ears, and it is that way with everything else they plant." Beverly Brown, "Mais: Sustainer of Life", *Maize*, Vol. 1 No. 1, 1983. Available from Word Weavers, Box 8742, Minneapolis, MN 55408.

[12] She is Mother Posop in Thailand, who is said to be pregnant when the grain is ripening. *Pacific and Southeast Asian Cooking* by Rafael Steinberg, Time Life Books, pp. 154-155.

IV. SOYFOODS

The Political Palate focused on the great store of classic Western non-meat recipes, those of French and Eastern European cooks using many dairy products. While we also used Middle Eastern and a few Far Eastern inspired dishes, this new volume is more about adaptation. We have become interested in using Eastern staples in Western ways. While Western enthusiasm for soy foods began with the health food movement, until recently not much attention has been paid to development of Western recipes which would make full use of soy food potential as delicious additions to our menus.

In the East, soy foods are basic: Tofu, soft or firm, dried or frozen; Miso as daily breakfast or dinner soup in Japan; Tempeh satés in Indonesia. In this country we are frequently disappointed in these foods when the prime goal is to satisfy what is believed to be the dictates of good nutrition. Yet, more and more Americans are eating tofu in places other than Asian restaurants and buying it in their supermarkets with little notion of how delicious really fresh, well-made tofu can be, either in its natural state or as a base to Western inspired dishes. Nor is there any sense denying that soy foods offer inexpensive protein alternatives to those of us with lactose intolerance, those worried about cholesterol intake, those concerned with hormone and other additives to meats and poultry.[13] We want to give soy

---

[13] It must be noted here that recent researchers have shown that protein is quite adequate in most vegetarian diets regardless of concern for balancing legumes and grains. In fact, most Americans, including vegetarians, consume too much protein for good health. See "The Latest Thinking on Protein" by John and Mary McDougall, *Vegetarian Times*, August 1984, and "New Research on the Vegetarian Diet" by Jane Brody, *The New York Times*, October 12, 1983.

foods the gustatory respect they deserve. While we may continue to enjoy them in restaurants or abroad prepared in traditional ways, we should explore what delicious Western dishes can be made with tofu, miso, tempeh, and well-aged soy sauce.

Tofu is best known and most popular of the soy foods. We have found it to be a bland extender or base and an emulsifier in custards, patés and cheesecakes. Since it has no richness of its own, oil is necessary to make tofu recipes taste rich and creamy. Many Westerners do not realize that of all foods, tofu suffers most from age. The freshest, sweetest tofu is that which you make yourself. Next comes the loose tofu available in health food stores and Asian markets. Least desirable is vacuum-packed tofu from the supermarket. Once you buy it, use tofu as soon as possible. While refrigeration under a cover of water changed daily helps retard spoilage, good flavor depends on quick use. If you have more than you can use within a few days, freeze it. Although the texture will change and sweet flavor will be gone, frozen tofu is still usable cubed in soups, or fried crispy as a garnish. We find its changed texture desirable in some dishes such as our version of Choucroute Garnie (sauerkraut cooked in wine) and Sancocho.

Miso, fermented soybean paste, comes in a number of flavors. Most misos in health food stores in Japanese markets are red or brown. Recently white (shiro) miso has become available at local health food stores. You will find misos have a natural sweet saltiness that is very effective in many recipes. In this book when we say miso, we usually mean one of the red or brown types, such as aka, mughi or hatcho. Try several to see which you like best. Tightly covered and refrigerated, miso keeps almost indefinitely. Those with a classical cooking

habit can use red or brown miso as if it were *glacé viande*. Tiny amounts of miso are a substitute for anchovies or anchovy paste in Italian dishes. For example, bits of miso can replace minced anchovies to make a superior sauce for fried mozzarella. To a Westerner's vegetarian taste, miso makes possible old fashioned gravies and sauces. White miso in combination with nutritional yeast makes scrambled tofu delicious. More vegetarian cookbooks include miso recipes these days, but Shurtleff and Aoyagi's *Book of Miso* remains the most complete discussion of this complex and sophisticated food.

Tempeh, made from soy beans in mold-fungi, is a soy food with another set of possibilities. Since the whole soybean is fermented and encased in mold, it absorbs flavors and moisture, and then is best fried or grilled. Tempeh treated this way assumes a firm, meat-like texture and good flavor. We have used tempeh with a sweet sour sauce, as if it were pork; we've served it after marinating in white wine as "chicken" salad with mayonnaise and grapes; it substitutes for lamb stuffing in Syrian eggplant, or for wild duck with cranberries over wild rice. Tempeh is for those times you want hearty food. Be sure to season it assertively and use some souring agent (such as wine, lemon juice or vinegar). It usually seems to want coriander, regardless of what other flavorings are used; both garlic and ginger complement its rather strong natural taste. Sauteéing is *not* recommended. Tempeh needs high heat and crispness, as well as strong sauces to be at its best.

In general, well-aged shoyu or soy sauce (known until recently as tamari) makes a good soup base. Omit salt and substitute 1-2 tablespoons of tamari per quart of liquid for almost any soup favorite. Using the standard vegetables, we make a very creditable chicken soup with shoyu, and Portuguese Kale and Potato Soup that doesn't miss the sausage. Perhaps the best example of shoyu instead of stock is the French Onion Soup recipe in *The Political Palate*.

To see what can be done with tofu, try the recipes most popular at Bloodroot: Pumpkin Tofu Custard, Mushroom Walnut Paté, Blueberry Almond "Cheese" Pie, and Maple Rhubarb Tofu Mousse. Simplest and most classically derived from Eastern cuisine is the Marinated Tofu Salad. Miso gravy is a delicious staple to be kept on hand in your refrigerator. Also try the Scrambled Tofu made with white miso. Sweet and Sour Tempeh, Tempeh "Chicken" Salad, Tempeh Stuffed Baked Potato, Tempeh "Wild Duck" over Wild Rice, and Syrian Baked Stuffed Eggplant are favorite tempeh dishes.

Try the soy foods recipes in this volume. We're sure you'll think of translating your old favorites in similar ways, and we hope you'll write and tell us about new recipes you develop.

V. ON COLLECTIVITY AND WORK

Bloodroot is a collective. We have become stronger in our eight years of working in a women's space. Three of us have been here since the beginning. Losing one of our collective members this past year tested our strengths and made us consider carefully how we feel about work and our way of living, as well as how this intersects with feminism and our politics. We are told our longevity is unusual, and this seems to be so. Because losing someone we worked with for six years, someone whose vision had seemed so similar to our own is painful, it is important for us to consider what makes our way of life a continuing satisfaction for the three of us, while we understand that this may not be true for others.

Perhaps one reason it works for us is that the way we work and live is more whole than is generally possible; it is of a piece, organic. We live our work and work our lives. Our rewards are daily because we live what we believe. However, there is much that is very demanding about our work. It requires long hours in our place of business. While it is varied, it is also often pressured. Fortunately we like each other's company as well as the company of women who work with us part time. We continue to be fed by the ideas of other women[14]. As we work, we spend much of our time talking about books and the ideas in them. We're still glad for the garden in

---

[14] In 1983 we doubled our bookstore space to accomodate old and new volumes that continue to nourish our spirits. Just as in *The Political Palate*, we hope to whet your appetite for our favorite books by quoting from them, and you will find them listed in the bibliography at the end of this book.

the summer, as well as the rest from it in the winter. A heavy snowfall means serenity, knitting, refinishing furniture, or simply sitting and talking.

There is very little room in our lives for anything else but Bloodroot. Some of us reflect on the convent (or Beguine[15]) lives of women where each hour of the day was predetermined. It is a satisfaction to us to have removed from our lives much of what Mary Daly calls the presence of absence: for example, television, and much of the other "entertainment" patriarchy provides. Often we must forego feminist events. On rare occasions, when one of us dearly wants to hear a speaker or go to a women's concert, we can usually arrange it. We all wanted to go to the Women In Print Conference in Washington, D.C. in 1981, and took our vacation accordingly.

The longer we work in a space informed by women's values, the clearer becomes the discrepency between our lives and the culture at large. As a result, our judgments seem more clearcut to us. The more one withdraws from patriarchy and its ideas, the easier it is to see the destructiveness and fragmentation inherent in it. It is understandable that many women are suspicious of judgment-making since so many of patriarchy's judgments are used against women's best interests. It is hard to hold different values from those generally assumed by society. However, as Mary Daly has written in *Pure Lust:*

[15] "The Beguines" by Gracia Clark describes the collective and highly autonomous political, economic and social systems developed in cities by women from the twelfth through fourteenth centuries in Europe. *Quest,* Vol I, #4.

> . . . women who settle for a partial break from patriarchy while
> failing to sustain and further the feminist vision — for example, by
> combining non traditional life styles with male-identifed activism
> or tokenized professionalism — may be "liberated" from the onus
> of the incarnate male presence just sufficiently to lose touch with
> the real horrors of patriarchy. Thus even the conditions of
> physical separation/freedom, which are so important for the
> development of a radical feminist analysis, are — in the absence
> of rigorous Elemental thinking —converted into servitude to the
> patriarchal system. [16]

Women who perceive themselves as different or as
defiant are also demanding tolerance or support for
pornography, or what they see as a feminist "right" to
sadomasochism, not understanding that these reflect
phallocracy's growing contempt for women. As women
hesitate to make judgments lest we be judged, we
should consider Cheri Lesh's words:

> It is time to stop pointing fingers and making scapegoats. Time to
> look at something very hard and real. We are all crazy and weird
> about sex. Heirs to thousands of years of degradation and
> torture, of man as S and woman as M, of white as S and non-
> white as M, of God as S and human as M, of civilization as S and
> nature as M — who among us can claim immunity, who among us
> has not tasted the whip sting of poison in the honey, has not
> confused the slap with the caress? Sadomasochism is the basic
> sexual perversion of Patriarchy. [17]

Tolerance for the rights of pornographers or for SM
practices derive from general support for the values of
new and old religions and their current incarnation as
psychotherapies, whether the pop types such as EST or
the latest in gestalt and neo-Jungian, without
recognition that these are used by patriarchy to contain
women's legitimate rage and to destroy our memories

[16] Mary Daly, *Pure Lust*, p. 143.

[17] Cheri Lesh, "Hunger and Thirst in the House of Distorted
Mirrors", *Against Sadomasochism*, p. 202-203.

and hopes. See work by Florence Rush, Phyllis Chesler, Jeffrey Masson, as well as Mary Daly:

> Just as Naming passions involves identifying the agent and object . . . , so also an adequate Naming of feminism requires Naming the stoppers as well as the direction of this movement. All else is therapy, psychobabble, therapy, self-hatred, therapy, futility.[18]

Presumably many wish to live and work in an integrated fashion without oppressing others — a hard dream to attain — and very different from the ways we have been taught to live or what we are taught are appropriate and expected pleasures. We have all learned to separate our lives into divisions/fragments: work during week in order to be able to play during weekends; work to earn leisure time; work to earn money to buy things that are supposed to make us happy. Living for real in the present means giving up the plastic world we're used to. Most women have little choice or means to escape the fragmentation that patriarchy considers the norm. As a result, a token few women are rewarded with high salaries for meaningless work, some of it occasionally interesting, while the assumption is that *everyone's* life takes place after business hours, on weekends or vacations. We are trying to live differently. As Audre Lorde has written:

> . . . the lack of concern for the erotic root and satisfactions of our work is felt in our disaffection from so much of what we do. For instance, how often do we truly love our work?

> The principal horror of any system which defines the good in terms of profit rather than in terms of human need, or which defines human need to the exclusion of the psychic and emotional components of that need — the principal horror of such a system is that it robs our work of its erotic value, its erotic power and life appeal and fulfillment. Such a system reduces work to a travesty of necessities, a duty by which we earn bread or oblivion for ourselves and those we love. But this is tantamount to blinding a

[18] Daly, *op. cit.*, p. 206, Florence Rush, *The Best Kept Secret;* Phyllis Chesler, *Women and Madness;* Jeffrey Masson, *The Assault on Truth.*

painter and then telling her to improve her work, and to enjoy the act of painting. It is not only next to impossible, it is also profoundly cruel.

As women, we need to examine the ways in which our world can be truly different. I am speaking here of the necessity for reassessing the very quality of all the aspects of our lives and of our work.[19]

There is much about Bloodroot that is wonderful and beautiful. Yet the maintenance of it requires commitment, devotion and lots of hard work (as does any very small business, but particularly the restaurant business). But we do go further, because we love our reading and we talk while we cook. Both our way of life and our reading make us intensely aware of extremity: the extremity of women's lives, the earth's life. It means our beliefs, our actions, our behavior, are all part of this intensity, this consciousness of extremity. We choose this consciousness. We choose living fully as we work. We choose work we believe in. For us, this kind of work, living, and time spent is breath and blood.

[19] Audre Lorde, "Uses of the Erotic: The Erotic as Power", *Out & Out Pamphlet #3.*

FURTHER THOUGHTS ON WORK

At Bloodroot we know we are always fighting a battle between the destructive direction of the patriarchal world and the need to press on with the creative activity of our survival as feminists. Part of the work here is to provide ground for radical consciousness: the discovery of hope, the movement of courage, and the possibility of willing the Self to act with moral intelligence.

We want to create a context where women can make vital connections: the careful weaving and mending which must be done on a daily basis, so that we and other women can begin to heal ourselves and sense our wholeness. To hold on to some part of the truth of our lives and to have the strength of conviction to continue: this is our challenge. For persistence is rebellion.

Bloodroot is a space of intense focus, since much of the process of creating a physical/psychic space involves both conscious will and profound respect for different capacities and strengths. As we have grown, our vision has developed more muscle. One of the discoveries we have made is that when there is time and space to work together, the possibilities of real harmony grow.[1]

---

[1] As Mary Daly has written: "Chord as a verb means 'to harmonize together: Accord.' The word accord literally brings us to the heart of the matter, since it is derived from the Latin *ad* plus *cor,* meaning heart. At its heart/core, Stamina is accord/harmony." *Pure Lust,* p. 312.

We are learning to condense the time it takes to resolve some of the daily problems of living and working together. There is no time to therapeutize a decision because the work must get done. (Therapy is like processed food; it is our memories and experiences which are processed as we absorb the additives of the therapist's training.) Of course, the larger problems concerning important and deeper differences between us, such as class complexities, race consciousness, and Christian ethnocentrism, require a more intense struggle over a longer period of time to move toward change. But the process of moving through them is on going because our beliefs create a context enabling us to continue what we consider our life-long work.

Certainly the women's movement reflects this process as we journey into the eighties. As a movement, we face the complex dilemma of living our histories and futures in the challenged present. Sometimes we act intuitively on more than we know. Sometimes we know more than we can act on. Women who identify as feminists frequently demand the impossible from each other: partly because there aren't enough of us, partly because we are breaking old/new ground; and finally, because as women, (particularly those defined as other: physically challenged, old, of color, poor, lesbian) we have been living the impossible: we were not meant to be.[2] In response to this negation of existence there is a strong movement among women which is making itself known through the intentional focus on our differences. Certainly Third World feminism is creating a growing and complex body of various works written by women of color which is demanding and shaping future visions of the women's movement.

---

[2] Audre Lorde, "A Litany for Survival," *The Black Unicorn.*

One result is that many white feminists are slowly and painfully realizing that the silences, false guilt, and distortions of racism created by patriarchy have prevented us from knowing an essential truth: safety in separation is our greatest danger. As Betsey Beaven wrote in *Womanews*, March, 1983:

> Part of the destructiveness of racism which operates daily in white women's lives is the power they hold in deciding whether or not they wish to hear the voices of women of color. In the women's movement of the 1980's, our actions, and our movements (particularly those of us who are white feminists) demand conscious resistance to our own ignorance. What white women have been taught, in a predominantly white Christian culture in North America, we as feminists have learned all too well. We need to move inside our ignorance and look at the weight of history to find out what we do not or have refused to acknowledge . . . we need to lead ourselves out of old patterns — familiar places of defensive fear and illusionary passivity. Our actions are not to "make up" for a past (with the sometimes paralyzing raw edge of guilt) but to *make up* a future where all women can take the journey together. Our task is not simple. There is a lot of work to be done. It seems we must do nothing short of thinking with our hearts.

And yet there are present dangers. Given our complex state of oppression as women, we fail each other all the time. There are good women, strong women, not speaking to other good women, strong women. And because of our desperate silences, it is easy to believe that in the end women will always betray each other. For betrayal takes place among friends, not enemies. Without some larger sense of the origins of our false separations, we will repeat the deadly patterns of self-destruction we have all learned so well.

There are many urgent questions. How do we determine when to be fair and when to be loyal and where do the truth of the two meet? How do we distinguish between accusations meant to destroy and anger which informs our integrity? How do we create a context for radical

communication which is imperative for our survival as a movement? We must not be afraid to make informed judgments, provided we distinguish between the authoritarian puritan ways of the fathers and the amazon sense of honor, as Anna J. Hearne as suggested. Moreover, the quality of loyalty must be reclaimed as a central focus for our movement:

> Loyalty is an Instinctive and Whole Heart bonding with Truth. A bonding which takes account of the Integrity of your Self, the Integrity of the Other, and the Integrity of the Whole. It is like Love, a minor miracle. Yet it is not too much to ask, for it is such as trees do, flowers do, and the Earth herself does all the time. And does so naturally . . . Loyalty demands that having bonded with Truth we act upon it. Act upon it not only in political and dramatic circumstances but in personal and mundane ones. Act upon it not only in situations between us and our Oppressor but in *situations between ourselves* . . . We have re-acted against our Self-destructive Loyalty to men with the realization that we must be generally Loyal to women. To ourSelves. But ultimately Loyalty is not a general quality. It is a specific one and a personal one. The Spirit of Loyalty can be generally felt for the Spirit of Women. But the Flesh of loyalty is Personal and Individual choices and actions made selectively wherein the Spirit of Woman is most honored.[3]

Thus loyalty is a quality whose source lies in the heart and as such must be felt in the bones. In a time when our personal and political lives as women are increasingly jeopardized, when the earth is held hostage by computerized nuclear weapons, the vital and loyal connections we have made with each other must be encouraged to grow. As feminists, we need more than to merely survive the daily devastations imposed upon our lives; we need to give life to our dreams.

[3] Anna J. Hearne, "Loyalty; The Lost Quality" *Womanspirit*, Winter Solstice, 1980, p. 56-57.

For us at Bloodroot, the most important truth lies in the act of our bonding and creating together. While our lives are sometimes seen as confining, for us the reality of our *being* together is the primary force of our creativity and continuance. At Bloodroot, we have begun the process of knowing what we don't want and what we don't need, and this allows us to seek what is possible. As Audre Lorde has written of both these states:

> For as we begin to recognize our deepest feelings we begin to give up of necessity being satisfied with suffering, self-negation, and the numbness which so often seems like their only alternative in our society . . . For once we begin to feel deeply all the aspects of our lives, we begin to demand from ourselves and from our lives, pursuits that feel in accordance with that joy which we know ourselves to be capable of . . .[4]

Our relationship to the earth and her creatures is the same relationship we must have with each other as sisters: when we hurt the earth we hurt each other; when we create with the earth we create with each other. Like birds close to the ground listening for movement, we must listen to each other to discover our magic. And there is magic, running like an underground stream, whose current flows and connects us all with the movement of women making revolution. We must protect and become our visions, for they are what is most sacred.

[4] Audre Lorde, *Uses of the Erotic: The Erotic as Power*, Out and Out Books, 1978.

"LAS VIAJERAS"

What follows is a children's fable in Spanish. It is not a coincidence that the creatures bear some biographical resemblance to us at Bloodroot. En Español, their journey seems more magical and more amusing. After all "una roca grande" does have more music in it than "a big rock." Those of you who don't understand Spanish should find a friend who does.

La cabra y la tortuga son amigas. Ellas suben las montañas juntas. Algunas veces, la cabra lleva a la tortuga en su espalda. Juntas descubren tantas maravillas. Ellas aprenden a comprender mucho a cerca de la tierra. A veces, se esconden debajo de una roca grande y allí almuerzan. Ambas aman mucho la tierra, las flores y los árboles, el mar y el cielo. Muchas veces, ellas miran a las nubes flotando.

Un día la cabra dijo, "Mira! En las nubes hay un ave pequeña, azul y rápida. Que linda!"

La tortuga la miró y exclamó, "Ven baja, ven baja! Tu eres maravillosa. Ven con nosotras. Caminaremos alrededor del mundo." El ave bajó y se posó sobre la oreja de la cabra.

"Bueno. Vámonos," ella dijo. Y ellas andubieron y andubieron todo el santo día. Por la tarde, ellas llegaron en frente de una caverna grande.

"Qué vamos hacer mis amigas?' preguntó la cabra. "Está muy negro allí adentro." Ella rodó sus ojos hacia arriba. Ella teniá un poquito de miedo y tambien mucha curiosidad. "Yo deseo saber que hay allí adentro."

La tortuga pensó en lo que ella dijo. "Entonces, entraremos muy cuidadosamente."

El ave pequeña voló hacia abajo y arriba con mucha agitación. "Sí, sí. Vamos! Esta es una aventura importante."

Así, las tres amigas entraron juntas en la caverna. Estaba muy oscura. La tortuga dijo bajito, "Por cierto, debemos ser prudentes." Así, ellas andubieron lentamente y con mucha atención. De pronto, la cabra se detuvo.

"Hay algo tibio y peludo cerca de mi pata delantera izquierda. Y se mueve!" Las tres amigas no hicieron ruido. Al poco tiempo hubo un gruñido y un bufido.

"Qué pasa?" algo pregunto.

El ave dijo, ""Qué es eso? Usted qué es?"

"Soy una osa."

"Cielos! Podemos mirarte? Ven afuera!"

"Sí, en un momento. Yo me muevo muy despacio." La osa se sentó y se paró lentamente. Entonces todas las criaturas salieron de la caverna.

Afuera, la tortuga miró pensativamente a la osa. "Ella es grande y solitaria," se dijo. "Tal vez ella quiera venir con nosotras."

El ave, volando alrededor de la osa dijo, "Que pieles mas admirables, son pieles carmelitas y dulces. Ven con nosotras! Nosotras exploramos él mundo."

La cabra cabrioló. "A lo mejor, tenemos una nueva amiga," dijo ella y chocó contra la osa un poquito.

La osa se rascó su cabeza y dijo, "Sí, estoy sola. Quizas vaya con ustedes."

Así las tres amigas encontraron la cuarta.

Esa noche, las cuatro amigas durmieron debajo de las estrellas cerca de un arbol grande. Por la mañana, ellas continuaron el viaje. Juntas caminaron a lo largo del bosque comiendo las bayas y hojas y ocasionalmente algunos insectos. Despues de muchos días caminando, vieron un río vasto. El sol estaba brillando y sintieron calor. Por eso, la osa se metió en el río a nadar. El ave se posó en su cabeza y se dio un paseo. Mientras tanto, la tortuga se sumergió y salió cerca de una roca plana, allí reposó. En la orilla del río, la cabra salpicó agua haciendo mucho ruido.

Mas tarde dejaron atras el río y continuaron su viaje. Ellas andubieron muchos días aprendiendo tanto acerca de la naturaleza y de la vida. Un día ellas llegaron a donde tres caminos se encontraban. La osa preguntó, "Ustedes siguen adelante, verdad?"

"Sí, sí. Ese es nuestro camino. Tenemos mucho que ver y hacer juntas," el ave respondió.

"Pero yo debo irme por el izquierdo," dijo la osa. "Quiero estar sola otra vez. Ustedes tienen que dejarme."

"Eso es lo que tú quieres?" la tortuga preguntó.

"Sí, tengo que buscar mi propio camino," dijo la osa.

La cabra se separó un poquito y dijo, "Qué lástima. A todas nos duele mucho que te vayas."

"Sí, mucho," la ave dijo bajito.

Así, la osa se fue por el camino izquierdo y las otras siguieron adelante. De este modo las cuatro amigas fueron tres otra vez.

Y así las tres continuaron su viaje sin la osa.

We have chosen each other
and the edge of each others battles
The war is the same
if we lose
someday women's blood will congeal
upon a dead planet
if we win
there is no telling
we seek beyond history
for a new and more possible meeting.

"Outlines"
Sister Outsider
Audre Lorde; Crossing Press

GLOSSARY

Achiote or Annatto — Rusty red dried seed which colors cooking oil bright orange yellow and imparts a delicate flavor.

Agar-agar — Also known as kanten. Available as strips or as flakes, it is the standard cultural growing medium for biological research and for orchid seedlings. It is a seaweed. We use it in flake form. It should not be stirred until it has softened in cold liquid and then brought slowly to a simmer. Don't boil. Once it simmers, stir occasionally until it appears to have dissolved. Agar-agar "sets up" at room temperature. It is an excellent substitute for gelatin (an animal product).

Alfalfa Sprouts —Easiest sprouts to raise in a kitchen garden. A jar with a screen and rubber band is all you need. Soak a few tablespoons of alfalfa seed a few hours in water to cover. Drain well, place in a dark place (such as a cupboard over a sink) and rinse twice daily. In three days they will be ready. Half a day on the windowsill will make them green. Then refrigerate.

Arame — In Japanese, arame means "the rough maiden." It is a social plant which grows in association with two other seaweeds, hiziki and ecklonia. See *Cooking With Sea Vegetables* by Sharon Ann Rhoads and Patricia Zunic, Autumn Press, 1978.

Arrowroot — *Maranta arundinacea,* a delicate starch used to thicken gravies and desserts, derived from a West Indian water plant. Interchangeable with potato starch and cornstarch. Though more expensive, it is considered to be more nutritious by some, and to give more "clear and limpid" results, according to Julia Child.

Barley Malt — A grain syrup made from sprouting barley, then toasting and grinding it. This means of reducing a complex carbohydrate to a simple sugar results in subtle sweetener.

Beach Plums — *Prunus maritima,* a small wild tree which grows on the sea shores of the Northeast.

Brown Rice — You will find several kinds in your health food store. In our opinion, Lundberg short grain is an especially delicious, quality brown rice.

Cardamom — The tastiest cardamom comes in green pods available in Indian markets.

Carob — A powder or flour ground from the carob pod or locust bean. It is naturally sweet, low in fat and has no caffeine. It has a dark brown flavor and substitutes for chocolate, but lacks the characteristic bitterness chocolate lovers like.

Cavatelli — A shell shaped pasta with good texture, available fresh in some Italian markets.

Chili-Paste-with-Garlic — A very pungent and spicy paste available in small jars in Chinese markets. Must be refrigerated after opening.

Cilantro — The name for a pungent herb, *Coriandrum sativum,* available in Hispanic markets; Chinese parsley is the name for it in Asian stores. Widely used in many cuisines.

Daikon — Japanese white radish ("great root"), easily grown in home gardens. Freshly grated, it is considered to have digestive enzymes useful in the consumption of oily foods.

Dashi — Japanese cooking stock made with kombu and dried bonito (fish) flakes. We omit the fish flakes and find the kombu adequate.

Date Sugar — Ground dried dates, available in health food stores; a substitute, in this granulated form, for brown sugar, especially for struesels.

Dende Oil — Palm oil used in Africa and in Bahia, the northeastern part of Brazil. Yellow colored and strong flavored.

Elderberry Jam — This is our preferred jam, gathered from the wild or cultivated. Strong flavored fruits are delightful in soup or as jam.

Fennel — This plant resembles a plump celery and has an anise or licorice flavor. Feathery leaves are an herb for seasoning. The stalk requires an ice water soak before it is sliced thin as an appetizer. Or fennel may be cooked. See recipe index.

Fides — Very fine noodles used in Middle Eastern pilafs. Vermicelli is too thick to use as a substitute. Fides is the Greek word used; shehrieh is the Syrian for this noodle.

Filberts — Cultivated hazelnuts.

Filo — Tissue paper thin pastry sheets used extensively in Middle Eastern cooking. Usually brushed with melted butter, it can be brushed with oil instead. Filo must be dealt with quickly or it dries out and becomes too brittle to shape. Held between two sheets of waxed paper and under a dampened towel, it will retain its flexibility. Look for brands with no additives.

Garam Masala — A mixture of roasted and ground spices used in Indian cooking. As Maddhur Jaffrey points out, every home in India and Pakistan has its own handed-down-from-grandmother recipe. Be sure to see hers in *World of the East Vegetarian Cooking*.

Hoisin — A savory Chinese sauce made from beans and garlic. Purchase it in an Asian market in cans. Once opened, transfer to a jar and store in a refrigerator. This pungent sauce needs dilution in cooking or before use as a dip.

Hungarian Paprika — Besides "Spanish" paprika used more to color food than to season it, there is Hungarian paprika. Canned paprika called "Szeged" has excellent flavor. Or purchase loose paprika, choosing "sharp" or "medium rose" or a mixture of the two. Available from Roth & Co., 1577 First Ave., New York, NY 10028; or Paprikas Weiss, 1546 Second Ave., New York, NY 10028.

Koji — Japanese word for "starter". This is usually the mold named *Aspergilis oryzae* used in making miso, amasake, sake, etc.

Kombu — A seaweed of the *Laminaria* family which is the base for the Japanese cooking stock called dashi. Kombu contains glutamic acid, a natural flavor enhancer. MSG is an artificial imitator of kombu. To preserve flavor, wipe clean of white powdery substance; don't wash.

Lecithin — A natural extract of the fatty part of the soybean. It contains vitamins and minerals and emulsifies fats (keeps them dispersed).

Manioc Meal — A grainy flour-like meal made from cassava root. When toasted, it is called farofa.

Masa Harina — Corn flour.

Pappadums — Wafers made from a variety of legumes, sometimes with the addition of pepper or garlic. Purchase at an Indian grocery, cut in half, and deep fat fry. Pappadums are delicious snacks.

Paprika — See Hungarian Paprika.

Pesto — Finely chopped fresh basil, garlic, and olive oil. Traditionally includes nuts, such as pignoli or walnuts. We use a food processor to make ours up in basil season (Summer) and freeze. We add chopped nuts at serving time when desirable.

Plantain — These are related to bananas, but must be cooked before eating. Like bananas, they are sweeter when ripe; press gently to see whether they seem soft. They are difficult to peel: slice sections vertically through to do so. Available in Hispanic markets.

Potato Starch — A thickener, interchangable with cornstarch. See arrowroot.

Queso Blanco — "White cheese". Available in Hispanic markets, this delicious cheese is best for use in Mexican dishes such as enchiladas. Mozzarella can be substituted for it if necessary.

Rice Wine Vinegar — Available in Asian markets, this vinegar is milder and sweeter than Western types.

Sesame Oil — Buy the strong flavored kind in an Asian market, not the type for sale in health food stores for recipes in this book. Expensive, a little goes a long way. The smell creates instant salivation.

Shehrieh — See Fides.

Shiitake — *Lentinus edodes,* the Golden Oak Mushroom, is now being cultivated in this country. It is also available dried. Its flavor is exceptional.

Shiro Miso — White miso is really light yellow. It is considered a Summer miso in Japan. Fermented for a shorter time, it is sweeter and less salty than red or brown misos.

Shoyu — Soy sauce brewed from soybeans, salt, wheat, and water. This traditional soy sauce has been called tamari until recently, to differentiate it from the chemicalized supermarket soy sauces. True tamari contains no wheat and is a by-product of miso making. In *The Political Palate* we used the term **tamari**; in this book we call the same sauce **shoyu**.

Sorrel — French sorrel, *Rumex acetosa,* is an easy perennial to raise from seed in your vegetable garden. Or, with patience, you can gather the tiny arrowhead shaped leaves of wild sheep sorrel (*Rumex acetosella,*) or wood sorrel (*Oxalis montana*) to get the appropriate tart flavor.

Summer Savory — *Satureia hortensis.* A delectable annual herb which should self sow after the first year you start it. Winter savory is a perennial with similar, but not as good flavor.

Sunchokes — *Helianthus tuberosus.* A native American perennial sunflower, less showy than garden varieties which grow four to ten feet tall. These plants are too invasive for your vegetable garden and would require a plot of their own. Dig the tubers, which grow in a circle around the root, after the first frost and store in the refrigerator. Sunchokes contain Inulin and are therefore supposed to be good for diabetics.

Tapioca — These pearl-shaped paste rounds are made from cassava root, as is manioc.

Tahini — Middle Eastern name for sesame paste. Health food sesame butter is different, and not a substitute. Chinese cuisine also employs sesame paste, also different in flavor from tahini. Use the right one for the respective recipe.

Tamarind — A fruit used as a souring agent in the way lemon is used. It has its own dark wonderful flavor, however. It can usually be bought as seeds pressed into one pound bricks in Indian and Hispanic stores.

Tofu — Soy bean curd. Tofu is made from soy milk (see recipe index) and then turned into curds and whey just as Western cheeses are made, except that the latter are usually coagulated by means of rennet, which is extracted from animals. Tofu is curdled by means of a "salt": either calcium sulfate (gypsum) used in China, or Nigari, bittern, derived from the sea (magnesium chloride plus other salts and trace elements). Or less desirably, tofu can be coagulated with lemon juice or vinegar. Tofu making kits are available for home use at most health food stores. The sweetest tofu is that you make yourself. See *The Book of Tofu* by William Shurtleff and Akiko Aoyagi, Ballantine, 1975.

Tomatillos — Originally used by the Aztecs and called Miltomatl. It is *Physalis ixocarpa;* relatives are Chinese lanterns, cape-gooseberries and ground cherries. Available fresh in some Latin American markets, this vegetable is specifically Mexican. Fresh tomatillos are decidedly superior to the canned for sauces.

CHAPTER 1   AUTUMN

～～～～～～～～～～～～～～～～～～

DESERTS

Take heed
guard your secrets
bury your treasures well,
your knives, your crystals,
your feathers and shells. . .
All your sacred things.
Like ancestors bones
they will be stolen,
pulverized into
instant powder to feed
white men's souls.

"Owl Woman"
Amber Coverdale Sumrall
Sinister Wisdom: A Gathering of Spirit
North American Indian Women's Issue

FRIED MOZZARELLA IN CAPER MISO SAUCE

This traditional Italian appetizer is better with the substitution of miso for anchovies.

1) Cut **1 lb. mozzarella** into 4 horizontal slices. Cut each slice diagonally in half. On a sheet of waxed paper, shake together ½ **c. flour,** ½ **t. salt,** and a **grating** of **pepper.** Set aside.

2) Fork beat **1 egg** thoroughly in a wide, shallow bowl. You will need **1-2 c. good bread crumbs** (no flavorings or additions) on a separate sheet of waxed paper. Of course, it is best to dry out your own homemade bread or to buy and dry out a good bread from an Italian bakery and crush it for crumbs.

3) Dip each triangle of mozzarella first into seasoned flour, then into egg, and then into bread crumbs. If crumbs don't stick well, especially at the edges, dip again in egg and back into the bread crumbs. Leave pieces of mozzarella on the bread-crumbed waxed paper to dry while preparing sauce.

4) Make Caper Miso Sauce: In a small pot stir together **1 Tb. red** or **brown miso** and **1 Tb. water** until blended. Add ¼ **c. dry white wine** and **1 Tb. capers.** (The cheapest capers can be found loose and salted in Italian markets. Be sure to wash these well in cold water if you use them instead of bottled capers.) Heat sauce gently. Chop about ¼ **c. straight leaf parsley** and slice **1 lemon** into wedges; set these aside.

5) When ready to serve, heat **2 Tb. sweet butter** in a
   frying pan until hot. Add mozzarella slices and brown
   well on both sides. Remove to plates, 2 triangles per
   diner. When all pieces are fried, turn off heat and add
   warm caper sauce to pan together with **4 Tb. sweet
   butter** cut into pieces. Blend this sauce well and
   spoon over mozzarella. Top each serving with parsley
   and lemon wedge.

Serves 4

*I remember always the feeling that it could continue
forever, this morning, this life. I remember the curl of
Muriel's finger and her deep eyes and the smell of her
buttery skin. The smell of basil . . . Each one of us had
been starved for love for so long that we wanted to
believe that love, once found, was all-powerful. We
wanted to believe that it could give word to my
inchoate pain and rages; that it could enable Muriel to
face the world and get a job; that it could free our
writings, cure racism, end homophobia and adolescent
acne. We were like starving women who come to
believe that food will cure all present pains, as well as
heal all the deficiency sores of long standing.*

Zami: A New Spelling Of My Name
Audre Lorde; Crossing Press

BROILED STUFFED MUSHROOMS

This recipe is even better tasting than the anchovy paste version in *The Political Palate*. Serve with ice water crisped, thinly sliced **fennel** and **Italian oil-cured olives**.

1) Use a fork to mash together ¼ **lb. cream cheese, 1½ t. lemon juice, 2 t. red miso,** and **1½ t. shoyu.** If mixture is too stiff, add a little **water.** Mince **1 scallion** and add to mixture.

2) Use a dessert spoon to scoop stems from **1 dozen large mushrooms.** Use fork to stuff mushrooms with cheese mixture. Sprinkle with **paprika.**

3) When ready to serve, broil only until tops are brown.

Appetizers for 6

All of us, set adrift in the twentieth century, are irretrievably grown up. All of us born after 1918; certainly all of us born after 1933; and especially those of us born after the explosions of 1945 — we are born old, knowing too much about Death.

About Men
Phyllis Chesler; Bantam.

TOMATO, CABBAGE & RICE SOUP

A good way to use up the last of the garden's tomatoes.

1) Finely dice **1 carrot, 1 leek,** well washed, and ½ **small bunch** of **celery,** including **leaves.** Saute in a soup pot in **1 Tb. oil** with ½ **Tb. whole fennel seeds.** When golden brown, add **2 c. water** and **1 Tb. pesto,** if you have it, otherwise add **1 t. dried basil.** Cover and simmer for 1 hour.

2) Coarsely chop **5 c. fresh tomatoes.** You need not skin them. Add to soup pot with ¼ **c. canned tomato paste.** Or alternately, add **1 qt. canned tomatoes with paste,** breaking up the tomatoes somewhat in the soup pot. Cut up ¼ **small cabbage** into 1½″ squares and add to simmering soup. Cook another 30 minutes. When cabbage and tomatoes seem done, add ⅓ **c. white rice** and cook 10 minutes more.

3) Season soup with **2 Tb. brown sugar, 2 t. salt,** and **1 Tb. lemon juice.** Taste and correct seasonings if necessary. Garnish each serving with **sour cream.**

Serves 6

PORTUGUESE KALE
& POTATO SOUP

Although this soup is traditionally served with Linguica,
a Portuguese sausage, we find the sausage quite
unnecessary. One of our Portuguese customers adds
cooked red beans to this soup.

1) Peel and chop **1 large Spanish onion** and turn into
   soup kettle. Add ⅓ **c. olive oil, 2 large cloves**
   crushed **garlic,** and **pinch hot pepper flakes.**
   Saute.

2) While onions are cooking, peel **3-4 medium size
   potatoes** and cut coarsely into 1½″ pieces.

3) Add potatoes to soup pot with **1 qt. water.** Bring to
   boil, then lower heat and simmer until potatoes are
   soft. Use a potato masher to crush potatoes a little.

4) Wash ½ to ¾ **lb. kale.** Washing with hot water will
   get rid of any aphids you may find on unsprayed kale.
   Remove tough stems, roll leaves up tightly, and shred
   with a French chef's knife.

5) Add kale to soup with **3-4 Tb. shoyu,** ½ **Tb. salt,**
   and **dash Tabasco.** Simmer until kale is done. Add
   freshly grated **pepper** and correct seasonings.

Serves 6

LEBANESE FAVA BEAN SOUP

1) If you can't find fava beans in a Middle Eastern market, you may find them in an Italian one. Or you could substitute lima beans. Soak **2 c. fava beans** overnight in **water** to cover. Skins on these large beans are very tough and must be pulled off before further cooking.

2) Finely chop enough **onions** to measure **1 c.** and mince **1 clove garlic.** Saute vegetables in a soup pot in **2 Tb. olive oil** until soft and golden. Add drained beans and **3 c. water.** Simmer, covered, until done, 1-2 hours.

3) Use a potato masher to crush beans in the pot. Soup will be quite thick. Add **3 c. water, 3 Tb. shoyu, juice** of **1 lemon, 1 t. salt,** freshly ground **pepper,** and **1½ c. plain yoghurt.** Return to a boil, stirring well. Correct seasoning.

4) Serve soup with chopped **straight leaf parsley** and a **lemon slice.**

Serves 6

"CHICKEN OF THE WOODS" DUMPLING SOUP

When you are fortunate enough to find *Polyporus sulfureus,* the delicious wild mushroom that tastes like chicken, you will probably have more than you can eat sauteed and creamed (see **Creamed "Chicken of the Woods"** in recipe index). So use the harder parts to make this "chicken" soup.

1) Put **3½ qt. water** to boil in a pot with following vegetables: **1 large onion,** unpeeled (skin will color the soup golden); **2 carrots,** scraped and cut into thirds; **3 outside stalks celery,** plus **inside leaves,** washed; **1 parsley root,** scraped, if available (this lends wonderful flavor to the soup) or **1 bunch straight leaf parsley** if root is not available; **1 parsnip,** scraped; **2 bay leaves;** ½ **bunch dill;** and the hardest parts of a **Polyporus sulfureus** (Chicken of the Woods) or **Polyporus frondosus** (Hen of the Woods). This broth is like the old "Stone Soup" story. It is really the vegetables and herbs that make the soup fragrant and flavorful. Simmer at least 1 hour or until vegetables are very soft. Pour into colander over another soup pot or large bowl and drain. Use a potato masher to push down on the vegetables in order to extract all flavor. Discard contents of colander. You should have about 3 qt. of broth.

2) Finish soup by adding ¼ **c. nutritional yeast** (available at health food stores) and ⅓ **c. shoyu.** Taste, and if needed, add more **shoyu** for a saltier

flavor. Scrape and cut **1 small bunch carrots** into matchstick pieces. Simmer in soup until barely done.

3) Make **dumplings** (knaidel): Separately simmer moderately hard **pieces** of **Polyporus** in **water** to cover about 30 minutes. Grind in food processor. Use a mixer to cream **5 Tb. sweet butter.** Add **3 eggs, 1 c. ground Polyporus, 1¼ t. salt,** a little **grated nutmeg.** Add ½ **c. straight leaf parsley,** chopped, and **1 c. matzah meal.** When well blended, chill for 1 hour.

4) Bring a pot of **salted water** to a boil. Moisten your hands and shape knaidel into 1″ balls. Poach, covered, in simmering water until dumplings float to the top, about 10 minutes. Drain and add to broth.

5) If soup seems too rich and strong, dilute with some dumpling poaching **water.** Chop a little **straight leaf parsley** and **dill** as a final garnish to the soup. Serve each diner 2 knaidel.

Serves 10

Keep them caged in zoos and circuses
Kill their babies for their snow white fur.
Pushing on to claim new logging land
Where will they go?
There's no more frontier.

"Who'll Save the Animals"
Woody Simmons
©Woody Simmons; Waffle Pub.

CELERIAC REMOULADE

1) Make **Beet Cabbage Relish** well in advance, at
   least one day ahead: Shred ½ **small cabbage** to
   make **3 c.** Sprinkle with **2 t. salt** and let stand 1 hour.
   Scrape clean and cook enough **beets** to make **2 c.**
   Grate cooked beets in a processor or with hand grater
   and combine with ¼ **c. cider vinegar, 3 Tb.**
   horseradish, ¼ **c.** chopped **scallions, salt** and
   pepper to taste. Squeeze cabbage dry of excess
   liquid and combine with beets. Refrigerate.

2) Peel **2 celery roots** (celeriac). Cut into matchstick
   pieces, much like french fries. Simmer in very little
   water in a stainless steel pot. Add **juice** of ¼
   lemon. Be careful not to overcook the celery root. It
   should be firm but tender when done. Remove root
   from liquid with slotted spoon and refrigerate, saving
   liquid.

3) Make **Seed Mayonnaise:** Grind together ½ **c.**
   sesame seeds, ½ **c. sunflower seeds, 1 Tb.**
   caraway seeds, using small coffee mill if you have
   one. Put ground seeds in food processor with **juice** of
   1 lemon, 1 small garlic clove, ¼ **lb. tofu, 1**½
   Tb. prepared mustard, and **1 Tb. miso.** Turn
   machine on and slowly add ½ **c. vegetable oil.** Add
   enough of the reserved celeriac broth to achieve a
   good consistency. Taste for miso, mustard and lemon.
   Fold in **2 Tb.** chopped **straight leaf parsley.**

4) On a bed of **lettuce,** make 2 thin crescents of Beet
   Cabbage Relish. Arrange celeriac in center with Seed

Mayonnaise on top. Garnish with strips of **green pepper** and **daikon** or radish slices. Drizzle with **Vinaigrette** (see following recipe).

Serves 6-8

VINAIGRETTE

1) In a jar or bowl combine ⅓ **c.** good quality **wine vinegar,** ½ **t. salt** and ½ **t.** good quality **prepared mustard** (we use Kosciusko). Shake or whisk together thoroughly.

2) Add **1½ c. oil** (we use a blend which is 25% olive oil, 75% pure vegetable oil) and freshly ground **pepper.** Shake or whisk again until well blended.

This window makes a perfect frame
For New England leaves like painted rain
They hold me as I hold this train
All shadows on a dime.

"Shadows On A Dime"
Ferron
Shadows On A Dime
Lucy Records, Penknife Productions, Ltd.
© Nemesis Publishing, 1984.

RUSSIAN POTATO
& SAUERKRAUT SALAD

1) Make **Mustard Vinaigrette:** Combine ⅓ **c.** good
   quality **wine vinegar, ½ t. salt,** and **2 Tb.
   prepared mustard** (we use Kosciusko). Whisk
   together thoroughly. Add **1½ c. oil** (we use a blend
   of 25% olive oil, 75% pure vegetable oil) and lots of
   freshly ground **pepper.** Whisk again until blended.

2) Peel and dice **5 potatoes, 2 carrots,** and **2 beets.**
   Boil each separately until tender. Drain. Chill beets.

3) Combine carrots and potatoes in a bowl. Add enough
   mustard vinaigrette to coat generously. Add ½ **lb.
   sauerkraut,** drained and lightly squeezed, **3** diced
   scallions, 1 small diced **cucumber,** and **3 Tb.**
   chopped **fresh dill.** Mix well and chill.

4) Arrange cold potato salad on a bed of **Boston
   lettuce,** garnish with chilled beets, **onion** slices, and
   diced **apples.** Add extra vinaigrette to each salad.

Serves 4-6

*On weekdays they lived on black bread, an occasional
egg, and the "Jewish fruits" — potatoes, onions,
cucumbers, beets, cabbage.*

Rivington Street
Meredith Tax; Jove

CREAMED
"CHICKEN OF THE WOODS"

A wild mushroom dish. See also **"Chicken of the Woods" Dumpling Soup** in recipe index.

1) Be sure you have correctly identified your mushrooms. While most large, tree-trunk-growing mushrooms are not poisonous, most also remain woody and inedible after cooking. When either *Polyporus sulfureus* (Chicken of the Woods) or *Polyporus frondosus* (Hen of the Woods) is fresh, soft and juicy, you will have excellent eating. Sometimes you will find one that is tough at its center, but tender at the edges. Trim off edges or use the whole mushroom, depending on its condition. Cut into 1" pieces.

2) Heat **sweet butter** in a frying pan and add cut-up mushrooms. Cook over high heat. Mushrooms will quickly absorb any amount of butter you add to the pan, so be careful not to add too much, just enough to fry mushrooms to light brown. Pour in **cream,** light or heavy to your taste, and cover pan. Stew mushrooms about 5 minutes. Add more **cream** if needed or reduce liquid in pan if too much sauce remains. Add **salt, pepper,** and **lemon juice.** Now chop **straight leaf parsley** and add. Serve over **rice, noodles** or on **toast.**

GRILLED FRESH SHIITAKE MUSHROOMS WITH PASTA & PEPPER TOMATO SAUCE

Large Japanese Shiitake mushrooms, *Lentinus edodes*, sometimes called Golden Oak Mushrooms, are now being commercially grown in this country. Their rich flavor justifies spending money for them when you can. We like to prepare them in this simple fashion as a garnish to a pasta dish.

1) Make **Pepper Tomato Sauce:** Clean and slice **8 frying peppers,** red ones if possible. Slice **1 very large onion.** Heat **3 Tb. olive oil** and **2 t. hot pepper flakes** in a pot, and fry peppers with onions over high heat until they wilt and begin to brown. Well browned vegetables give a natural sweetness to this sauce.

2) Add **29 oz. plain tomato sauce** to the pot with ¼ **c. shoyu.** Rinse tomato sauce can with an equal amount of **water** and add to pot. Add ½ **can red wine, salt** and **pepper** to taste. Simmer 20 minutes.

3) Finish sauce with **3 Tb. pesto,** if available. Chop ½ **bunch straight leaf parsley** and add. Sauce should be thin and not very tomato tasting. Thin with equal parts **water** and **wine** as necessary.

4) Cook **2-3 lb. linguine** until just done. Drain well. We prefer imported linguine.

5) Just before serving, heat broiler very hot. Use **1 Tb. olive oil** to lightly grease a shallow pan. Slice **1 lb. Shiitake mushrooms** in strips and arrange cap side down in the pan. Sprinkle with **kosher salt** and drizzle with very little **olive oil.** Broil without turning until mushrooms smell wonderful and edges begin to brown.

6) Arrange pasta on a serving platter. Top generously with sauce, sprinkle more chopped **parsley** over the top, and place grilled mushrooms on top of platter.

Serves 6-8

And how many berries did Grandmother's hands gather! After the first berry harvest, she would bake a pie . . . Grandmother stitched a small basket from birch bark for me so that I could carry home what I had collected. She treated the berry bushes carefully: she did not pick them clean but left some for other berry lovers to enjoy . . .

. . . And when I wander the forest collecting mushrooms, berries, and herbs, I feel the harvest in my blood. When summer arrives, I stitch a basket from birch bark and go off to the woods. Those who remember her tell me, "You take after your grandmother."

"My Grandmother"
Z. Sinaneft
Women and Russia: Feminist Writings
from the Soviet Union
Ed. Tatyana Mamonova; Beacon Press

PASTA PUTANESCA

Named for Italian streetwalkers, this sauce is always made
with olives; other ingredients are intended to make a
savory, well-flavored sauce.

1) Use a small knife, preferably with a curved blade, to
cut ⅔ **c. green cured olives** and **3 Tb. black
cured olives** away from their pits. You will find olives
like these at Italian groceries. Set aside. Thinly slice
1 large onion, 2 seeded **Italian green peppers,**
and **1 head fennel.** Chop and save the feathery
leaves of the fennel, but discard the hard upper green
part of the stalks.

2) Make Putanesca Sauce: In a large saucepan heat
3 Tb. olive oil. Add onions, peppers, and fennel
with a **pinch** of **hot pepper flakes** and **1-2
cloves** chopped **garlic.** Saute gently about 5
minutes or until vegetables have wilted and are
turning golden. Add **3 Tb. tomato paste** and
cook, stirring, another 5-10 minutes. Now add ⅔ **red
wine** and **1 large can** (2 lb. 3 oz.) **plum
tomatoes.** Use a wooden spoon to coarsely break
up tomatoes. Simmer, covered, 45 minutes.

3) Sometimes we find wild edible boletes to add to this
sauce; lacking them, we use shiitake mushrooms, the
Japanese Golden Oak mushroom now in cultivation
here. Their strong flavor is similar to the Italian
boletes. If neither is available, leave mushrooms out.
Slice and fry ⅔ **c. mushrooms** in **2 Tb. olive oil** in
frying pan and add to sauce. Finely chop ½ **bunch
straight leaf parsley** and add. Taste for salt.

Depending on the saltiness of the olives, you may need to add **1-2 t. salt.**

4) For best flavor and mindful of the putanesca theme, fresh cavatelli is the best pasta to use. In a large amount of **boiling salted water,** cook **1½ lb. cavatelli** or other pasta until just done. Taste to be sure. Drain well.

5) As a final garnish, steam **1 bunch broccoli,** tops only, divided into rosettes, until barely done and still bright green. Spoon sauce over pasta and top platter or individual plates with broccoli rosettes. Serve with freshly grated **Parmesan cheese.**

Serves 5-6

I'm going to grow rage like a tomato,
kind of a great red fruit could
wreck bridges or bring down sauce
on half the city . . .

No apologies, explanations, excuses,
nothing but me, my tomato, my rages,
my name,
my name.

"Tomato Song"
The Women Who Hate   Me.
Dorothy Allison; Long Haul Press

CHOUCROUTE GARNIE

Traditional Alsatian sauerkraut is garnished with
smoked pork or bacon, sometimes with preserved
goose. We have chosen other garnishings, and expect
you will find that sauerkraut cooked in wine and served
with potatoes as satisfying a cold weather meal as we
do.

1) For the garnish, freeze **½ lb. tofu** overnight. When
we know we have more tofu than we can use while
fresh, we wrap the excess in foil and store in the
freezer so there is usually some available. Next day,
defrost and gently squeeze moisture from the tofu.
Dice. Cut **1 cake tempeh** (8 oz.) into dice.
Combine ⅓ **c. white wine** with **2 Tb. shoyu** in a
bowl. Add tofu and tempeh, turning often, to
marinate.

2) Drain **2 lb. sauerkraut** in a colander. Wash, drain,
and squeeze liquid out until as dry as possible. Chop
enough **onions** to yield **1 c.** Peel and dice **1 clove
garlic.** Saute onions in **2 Tb. oil** in a large frying
pan. Add garlic and ½ **t. crushed juniper
berries.** (These we collect fresh from juniper
bushes or red cedar trees. They can be purchased
dried in some fancy markets.) When onions are
softened and beginning to brown, add sauerkraut and
continue frying a couple of minutes. Peel **1 small
potato** and hand grate over frying pan (about ½ c.
grated potato). Turn heat to low and add **1 c. white
wine** (we use stale champagne), ¾ **c. water, 1⅓
Tb. shoyu,** and **1 bay leaf.** Cover and simmer 1
hour.

3) Meanwhile, heat **2-3 Tb. oil** in another frying pan
   until quite hot. Fry marinated pieces of tofu and
   tempeh, stirring constantly, until browned and crispy.
   It is best to do this in several batches. As each is
   done, add to the simmering choucroute. Any
   remaining marinade may also be added. Finish
   choucroute, if you like, by adding **1 Tb.
   kirschwasser** and simmer another 5 minutes.

4) Serve with **boiled potatoes,** buttered and
   sprinkled with **parsley.** Also serve **Glazed
   Carrots:** Cut **1 lb. carrots** into 1½″ lengths.
   Stew/saute in **½ c. water, 1 Tb. butter, 1 t.
   honey, ⅛ t. salt,** and freshly ground **pepper** until
   tender and browned.

Serves 6

Survivors run in my family
German, Jewish refugee
A Miracle of Chemotherapy
And now there's me.

"Survivors"
Laura Wetzler
Touch And Go; *Laura Wetzler Music.*

COLCANNON

This is a basic Irish dish which is well seasoned and surprisingly satisfying. Potatoes are sometimes combined with cabbage, sometimes with kale. We like to use both. For a complete meal, serve Colcannon with a side dish of rutabagas and carrots, as well as **Apple Chutney.**

1) Peel and quarter **8 medium potatoes.** Boil in **water** to cover until tender, but not falling apart. Drain in colander. Return to pot and shake over low fire until mealy. Mash potatoes with a fork, potato masher, or in a mixer. Add **2 Tb. sweet butter, 1 c. milk, salt** and **pepper** to taste. Set aside.

2) Finely shred **2 c. cabbage** and **2 c. kale,** well washed. Cover with **water** in a pot and bring to a boil, covered. Remove lid and boil uncovered 10 minutes. Drain well in a colander. Turn into frying pan with **2 Tb. sweet butter.** Fry for about 5 minutes until slightly browned. Add to mashed potatoes. Colcannon is now ready to be served as is, or can be reheated in a 350° oven.

3) Dice **1 bunch carrots** (about 2 c.) and an equal amount of peeled **rutabagas.** Add just enough **water** to steam vegetables. Add **2 Tb. sweet butter, salt** and **pepper** to taste. Cover and cook until barely done. Now uncover pot and raise heat, stirring, until vegetables are glazed and slightly brown.

4) Serve Colcannon with buttered carrots and rutabagas topped with **Beer Gravy** and diced **scallions.** Serve **Apple Chutney** on the side. See following recipes.

Serves 4

It is a consciousness of her own Otherness that enables a woman to know the other Others. Since women are the primal Other within patriarchy, the universal caste system on this planet, women have the primal Possibility of Allocentric knowledge that can embrace our Selves and touch other Others. Wild women, then, are Shape-shifters whose Other-knowledge shields us from the framers and pulls/attracts us into further transformations.

Pure Lust
Mary Daly; Beacon Press

BEER GRAVY

This variation on **Miso Gravy** (see recipe index) contains more beer than the original and also makes use of nutritional yeast, a product available at most health food stores, which has a flavor remarkably like chicken bouillon. Do not confuse it with brewer's yeast which has a bitter taste. See which miso gravy you prefer.

1) Mince **1 small onion, 3 large mushrooms,** and **1 large clove garlic.** In a saucepan melt **2 Tb. butter** and ¼ **c. cooking oil.** Saute vegetables until lightly browned.

2) Add ⅓ **c. whole wheat flour** and ⅓ **c. nutritional yeast.** Cook over low heat, stirring occasionally, about 10 minutes.

3) Add **12 oz. beer,** any inexpensive kind, or for especially full-bodied flavor, try **Guinness Stout.** Whisk gravy well, adding **1 ½ c. water,** ½ **t. dried thyme,** crumbled, ½ **t. dried basil, 2 t. tomato paste, 1 t. honey, 2 Tb. cider vinegar, 2 bay leaves, 3 Tb. shoyu,** and **2 Tb. red** or **brown miso.**

4) Cover and simmer approximately 20 minutes, stirring occasionally. If gravy becomes too thick, use **water** to reach desired consistency.

Yields 4 cups

APPLE CHUTNEY

Chutney will keep at least a month in a covered container in the refrigerator.

1) Peel, core and dice **4 c. apples.** (We prefer Staymen Winesap, but any crisp cooking apple will do.) Coarsely chop **1 c. onions.**

2) Tie **1 t. mixed pickling spice** in a piece of cheesecloth. Grind **1½ t. mustard seeds** with a mortar and pestle or in a small coffee mill.

3) In a stainless steel pot combine the apples, onions, pickling spices, and mustard seed with **¾ c. seedless raisins, ⅔ c. dark brown sugar,** and **¾ c. cider vinegar.** Add a rounded ¼ **t. dry ginger** and ¼ **t. cayenne pepper.**

4) Bring mixture to a boil, stirring occasionally, then reduce heat and simmer for about 2 hours or until most of liquid has cooked away. Be sure to stir frequently during this time to avoid burning.

5) Remove the cheesecloth with pickling spices. Cool, chill. Serve with **Colcannon.**

Yield about 2 cups

NATIVE AMERICAN WILD RICE DINNER

In an attempt to explore native American foods and flavors, we developed this harvest menu using some ingredients quite foreign to this land: tempeh, shoyu, wine. Though native Americans used meats on occasion, they used no dairy products. Nut butter provided enrichment. If you decide to prepare the whole meal as we do, you will have to start the **Dried Corn Succotash** first, then the **Wild Rice,** make **Nut Butter** and **Hazelnut Corn Cakes,** then put up **Sunchokes** to bake (they take 1-1½ hours). Then prepare **Tempeh "Wild Duck".** We also serve a wedge of steamed **pumpkin** or **squash,** as well as a **Watercress Sunchoke Salad** with this meal. Recipes are designed to serve 6.

We made the fires. We are the fire-tenders. We are the ones who do not allow anyone to speak for us but us. Spirit. Sisterhood. No longer can the two be separated.

Introduction
Beth Brant
Sinister Wisdom: A Gathering of Spirit
North American Indian Women's Issue

TEMPEH "WILD DUCK" WITH CRANBERRIES

1) Cut **2 cakes tempeh** (1 lb.) in half horizontally to yield 2 thin layers. Then divide lengthwise into thirds, finally crosswise into strips. Set aside. Dice **2 medium onions** and **4 large celery stalks** plus **leaves**.

2) Pour **2 Tb. oil** in a frying pan and saute vegetables and tempeh over high heat, stirring constantly. Add **2 cloves** crushed **garlic**, ¾ **t. marjoram**, and ½ **t.** crushed **juniper berries**, if available. Fry mixture until all is evenly browned, adding more **oil** if necessary. Add **1⅓ c. red wine, 1⅓ c. water, 3 Tb. wine vinegar, 3 Tb. shoyu**, and ¼ **c. maple syrup.** Finally, add **1 lb. (5¼ c.) cranberries,** first picking them over to remove stems. Cover and simmer until cranberries are just done. Season with freshly ground **pepper** and serve over **wild rice,** or for a less expensive meal, serve over cooked **brown rice.**

Serves 5-6

SUCCOTASH

This dairy free succotash is more delicious than ones made with milk or cream. However, you will need to find dried corn. We found ours in Casa Moneo, a store on 14th Street in New York specializing in South American foods.

1) Put **1 c. lima beans** in a pot cover with **water,** and soak overnight. Next day, rinse, cover with fresh water and cook, covered, 1-2 hours until tender. Check often to be sure there is enough water.

2) In a separate pot cover **1 c. dried corn** (either white or yellow), with **water** and cook, covered, for about 1 hour or until tender. Be sure there is enough water to prevent sticking or burning.

3) In a frying pan saute **1 medium onion,** diced, and **1 green pepper,** chopped, in **1 Tb. oil.** When golden brown, combine corn, limas, onion and pepper in one pot. Add **2 t. salt, 1 Tb. nut butter,** and freshly ground **pepper.** Add **water,** if needed, for a creamy consistency. Reheat when necessary.

Serves 6-8

WILD RICE

Bring **3½ c. water** to a boil. Meanwhile, wash **1½ c. wild rice** in a strainer under running water. Turn washed rice into boiling water, cover and reduce heat to moderate. Rice should be tender in 45-55 minutes. Use a steamer to reheat if necessary.

NUT BUTTER

Roast **½ c. hazelnuts** 5-10 minutes at 400°. Using a towel, rub off as many skins as you readily can. Turn into a food processor and pulverize very thoroughly. Add **3 Tb. oil, 1 scant t. maple syrup,** and ⅓ **c. water.** Mix well. Refrigerate. Nut butter does not keep more than a few days.

Yet the failure to examine heterosexuality as an institution is like failing to admit that the economic system called capitalism or the caste system of racism is maintained by a variety of forces, including both physical violence and false consciousness.

Compulsory Heterosexuality and Lesbian Existence
Adrienne Rich; Antelope Publications

HAZELNUT CORN CAKES

1) Pulverize ½ **lb. hazelnuts** in a food processor.
   Turn into a pot and add **2 c. water.** Simmer about
   30 minutes. Add **1 t. maple syrup, ½ c.
   cornmeal,** and **1 c. water.** Bring to a boil again.
   Let cool.

2) In a frying pan heat **2 Tb. oil.** Use a spoon to dip
   out cakes into hot pan. Fry until edges turn brown.
   Use a stiff spatula to scrape nut cake up. Turn over,
   flatten, and fry other side until brown. Repeat until all
   batter is used. These cakes can be served at room
   temperature or reheated briefly in the oven.

Yields about 15-18 small cakes

ROASTED SUNCHOKES

1) Put **6 sunchokes,** washed but not peeled, in a
   small pan and roast in a toaster oven at 375°-400° for
   1-1½ hours. When they are done, you will see signs of
   the sweet juices oozing out. To serve, cut in half and
   top with **Nut Butter.**

Serves 6

WATERCRESS SUNCHOKE SALAD
WITH WALNUT OIL

For each diner, make a salad of equal parts **Boston lettuce** and **watercress.** Top with slices of **onion.** In a jar combine **1 part cider vinegar** with **3½ parts walnut oil, salt,** and freshly ground **pepper** to taste. Shake well. When ready to serve, top with sliced **sunchokes** and salad dressing.

White woman go back home
you do not understand white justice broke
our treaties and stole our sacred land.
We will not beg or bargain with those
who steal and lie
if there's justice to be done
its we who will decide

"Manitoba"
Strong Singers
Cathy Winter and Betsy Rose; Origami Enterprises

SEITAN WITH
STIR FRIED VEGETABLES

Wheat gluten is an ancient Asian use of wheat flour as a meat substitute. You may be able to find it ready prepared in Asian or health food markets, as we do, or you can make your own, using the following recipe from our friend Ann Alves. Our seitan comes from our tofu makers, The Bridge, Middletown, CT, where it is packed in a soy-ginger flavored broth.

1) Gently squeeze broth from **1 lb. seitan,** using your hands, and reserve. Cut seitan into thin strips. Set aside seitan and broth. You will need **3½ c. liquid.**

2) Cut ¾ **lb. carrots** into pieces, using the Chinese roll cut if you are familiar with that technique. By slicing diagonally through the carrot with your knife and then rolling the carrot part way, pieces come out in an asymmetric shape. Cut **2 large red peppers** into strips, and slice **3 c. mushrooms.** Also peel and roll cut enough **broccoli stems** to measure **4 c.** This recipe uses usually discarded broccoli stems to very good advantage.

3) In a wok or large frying pan heat **2 Tb. oil.** When hot, add vegetables, but not seitan. Turn vegetables constantly until edges are beginning to brown nicely. Add ½ **t. dried ginger, 3 cloves** crushed **garlic,** and sprinkle lightly with **salt.** When browning is adequate, turn off the fire.

~~~~~~~~~~~~~~~~~~~~~~~~~~~~~~~~~~~~

4) In a bowl stir together the **3½ c. seitan liquid** (or an equivalent amount of **water** and **2 Tb. shoyu**), **3 Tb. cornstarch, 2 Tb. shoyu, 1 Tb. Chinese sesame oil,** ⅓ **t. Chinese chili paste with garlic,** and **1 t. honey.** Pour over mixture in pan and turn on heat. Stir until gravy is thickened and clear. Add seitan strips and heat thoroughly before serving.

5) Serve over **brown rice** garnished with sliced **scallions.**

Serves 6

"They are not perfectly formed," she said. "Nothing steadies them. They are bloodless. They spill their seed upon the ground and are empty as husks. Always they are hungry to be filled with life, yet they fear it. The Mother's blood frightens them. Then they are ashamed to show their fear. Like children, they pretend to be brave. Like children, they destroy what they cannot have. The life that will not flow through them, they spill out in rage. In the old time, they were in awe and could be gentled. Now they are all killers."

Ariadne
June Rachuy Brindel; St. Martin's Press

WHEAT GLUTEN & SEITAN

We buy our seitan from our nearby tofu dairy. This is our friend Ann Alves' recipe for her delicious home-made seitan. Seitan is very like beef stew in consistency. It can be very chewy, so cut pieces fairly small before serving in soups or stews. Use of gluten in China and seitan in Japan is ancient.

1) Combine **10 c. hard whole wheat flour** and **5 c. unbleached white flour** with **5½ c. water** and **1½ t. salt.** Form a dough and knead vigorously for about 20 minutes until dough is smooth and of "earlobe" consistency. Let dough rest 20 minutes.

2) Put dough in a large bowl and cover with **water.** Soak 20 minutes or longer, up to 4 hours, in a cool place.

3) Put bowl of dough in sink and knead to squeeze out starch. As water becomes milky, drain and add fresh, warm water. Dough will get soft and sticky; it will also form sinews and turn stringy, resilient and compact. This takes about 10 minutes. When water is almost clear, but all the bran (brown flecks) not gone, remove dough to a dish towel and continue to knead while excess water is absorbed.

4) Bring a pot of **water** to a boil. Drop pieces of dough into the pot and remove when they come to the top. This is gluten or kofu.

5) To produce seitan, cook gluten with seasonings in a
pot or a pressure cooker. For the latter, add ⅔ **c.
shoyu,** a **small piece** of **kombu** (dried seaweed),
and a **2″ knob** of **fresh ginger,** sliced, to the
pressure cooker with gluten and its cooking water.
Cook 1 hour under pressure. Bring the pressure
down rapidly, and add more **water, shoyu, ginger,**
and other herbs, such as **bay leaves,** if you like.
Simmer the seitan, which will have doubled in size,
for another hour. Or, for a firmer seitan, don't use the
pressure cooker, but simmer several hours in a soup
pot. Then uncover to let most of the liquid boil off.

*There is no state of being or act of will, including
lesbianism, that changes the circle: there is no state of
being or act of will that protects a woman from the basic
crimes against women as women or puts any woman
outside the possibility of suffering these crimes. Great
wealth does not put a woman outside the circle of crimes;
neither does racial supremacy in a racist social system
or a good job or a terrific heterosexual relationship
with a wonderful man or the most liberated (by any
standard) sex life or living with women in a commune in
a pasture.*

Right Wing Women
Andrea Dworkin; Wideview/Perigee

DIPPING SAUCES FOR STEAMED VEGETABLES & ROASTED POTATOES

In *The Political Palate* we wrote of this simple dish, in which potatoes roast in an oiled pan in the oven and carrots, broccoli, and cauliflower are briefly steamed. Serving these with a choice of dipping sauces makes a nice dinner. In addition to a **Mornay** (cheese) **Sauce** and a **Sour Cream Sauce,** we now also offer **Tofu** and **Miso Sauces.**

TOFU DIPPING SAUCE

1) Simmer **1 lb. tofu** in **water** to cover for a few minutes. Drain well.

2) Place in food processor: drained tofu, **3 Tb. gomahsio** (see recipe index), **1 t. fresh ginger,** grated, **3 Tb. shoyu, 3 Tb. rice wine vinegar,** and **1 Tb. honey.** Process until smooth. Season with **lemon juice** to taste. If you grow **mitsuba** (Japanese parsley), chop **2 Tb.** and add.

Yields about 1 c.

MISO DIPPING SAUCE

In a blender or processor combine ⅓ **c. white miso, 1 c. cashew butter, 1 small clove garlic,** and **1¼ c. water.** Process. Add more **water** if necessary. Season to taste with **shoyu** and **lemon juice.**

Yields about 1½ c.

GOMAHSIO

1) In a heavy skillet over medium high heat roast **2 Tb. sea salt,** stirring constantly until the chlorine odor is released. This takes about 1 minute. Transfer the salt into a stainless steel bowl.

2) In the same pot over medium high heat roast **1 c. sesame seeds,** stirring often, until light brown and fragrant.

3) Grind the salt and roasted seeds together with a mortar and pestle or by machine. We use a small electric coffee mill. Do not overgrind or you will have sesame butter.

Makes about 1 cup

MINCEMEAT BAKED APPLES

A dairy free and sweetening free dessert.

1) Marinate **3 Tb. raisins** in ¼ **c. apple jack brandy** (or **apple juice**). Cut **3 Tb. dried apricots** into small dice and add. Chop ⅔ **c. walnuts** and add with ⅓ **c. sunflower seeds**, ⅛ **t. cinnamon**, and a **dash nutmeg**. In a cup mash **1 Tb. red miso** together with ½ **Tb. water** and add to nut and fruit mix. Stir to blend well.

2) Peel 1" off top of **7 Rome Beauty apples** or other large baking apples. Use an apple corer to cut out the core without cutting through the bottom of the apple. Core widely to make a nice hole for the filling. Push nut and fruit filling firmly into each hole and line up apples in a baking pan.

3) Pour **5 Tb. apricot wine** or **dry sherry** over apples and into pan. Bake at 325° for 45 minutes.

4) Serve warm with **Tofu Vanilla Creme** (see following recipe).

Serves 7

TOFU VANILLA CREME

A dairy free dessert topping.

1) In a small pot simmer **½ lb. tofu** in ½ **c. apple juice** for 5 minutes.

2) Lift tofu out of juice and put into a food processor. Add **1 Tb. tahini, pinch salt, dash cinnamon, ¾ t. vanilla extract,** and ¼ **t. almond extract.** Turn machine on and add **3 Tb. salad oil.** Now add the apple juice from the pot. Puree thoroughly, scrape down sides of processor, and puree again. This sauce thickens up in the refrigerator, so it should seem thin. Taste. If the tofu you are using is very fresh, no sweetening will be needed. However, if it is not sweet enough, **1-2 t. maple syrup** may be added. On the other hand, if a very sweet apple juice was used, you may want to add a **few drops** of **lemon juice.** Tofu Vanilla Creme does not keep well and is best served within a day or two.

Yields approximately 1½ cups

MAPLE APPLE COBBLER

An improved version of the Apple Cobbler that appears in *The Political Palate*.

1) Preheat oven to 400°. In a mixer combine **3 c. unbleached white flour, ¾ t. baking powder,** and ¾ **t. salt.** While mixing add ½ **lb. sweet butter** cut into small pieces. Do not worry about overbeating. Remove from mixer and press about ⅔ of this "pastry" into a 9" x 12" baking dish.

2) Finely chop ½ **c. walnuts** and mix into remaining pastry with **2 Tb. date sugar** (available at health food stores). Set this "streusel" aside.

3) Peel, core, and slice **4-5 apples.** Press apple slices into pastry in pan. Pour ¾ **c. maple syrup** over slices and sprinkle lightly with **cinnamon.** Bake for 10 minutes.

4) Meanwhile whisk together in a large mixing bowl: **3 c. sour cream, 3 egg yolks,** and ⅔ **c. maple syrup.** Pour over apples in oven and top with reserved streusel. Sprinkle again with **cinnamon** and bake 30 minutes longer. Cobbler is done when streusel is lightly browned and there is a minimum of movement when pan is jiggled.

5) Serve warm with **heavy cream.**

Serves 12

PUMPKIN TOFU CUSTARD

This dairy free dessert is from Mike Gross. To make **Pumpkin Tofu Pie,** bake the custard mixture in a pie crust, but since we use butter in our pie crust, it would then not be dairy free.

1) You will need **1½ c. cooked Hubbard squash** or **pumpkin.** Put in food processor or blender with **1 lb. tofu, 2 Tb. tahini, ½ c. pure maple syrup, ¼ c. water,** and puree thoroughly. Preheat oven to 375°.

2) Add to processor: **¾ t. salt, ¾ scant t. cinnamon, ⅔ t. ginger, ¼ t. nutmeg, ⅛ t. cloves, ½ t. vanilla extract.** Taste and add more **maple syrup** if you like custard sweeter.

3) Pour into individual custard cups. Place in pan with water to come half way up sides of custard cups. Bake at 375° about 30 minutes.

4) Make **Coconut Cream** (a dairy free topping): Put **1 c. dried unsweetened coconut** in a blender with **1 c. hot water.** Blend thoroughly. Strain, squeezing coconut to release the cream. Discard coconut pulp. Store in refrigerator.

Serves 6

APPLE STRUDEL

A dairy free and sweetening free dessert.

1) Stew ½ **c. dried apricots** and ½ **c. dried apples**
   in **apple juice** to cover until quite tender. Puree in
   food processor, adding more juice if necessary to
   make a thick paste. Set aside.

2) Peel, core, slice, and dice enough **crisp, tart
   apples** to yield **6 cups.** (Stayman Winesaps are
   best if you can find them.) Turn apples into a bowl,
   add **1 c. currants, 1 t. cinnamon,** ½ **t. nutmeg,
   2 c.** finely chopped **walnuts,** ¾ **c.** chopped
   almonds, grated **rind** of **1 lemon, 1**½ **t. vanilla,**
   and enough of the apricot paste to sweeten the
   mixture.

3) You will need **1**½ **to 2 c.** of good quality **bread
   crumbs,** preferably home made. Open **1 lb.** of **filo**
   and stack about 8 sheets one on top of the other,
   brushing each with **walnut** or **safflower oil.** You
   will be using about ⅓ of the pound for each studel roll
   you will be making. Now sprinkle generously with
   bread crumbs. Add ⅓ of the apple filling to the long
   end facing you and roll up as tightly as possible.
   Carefully cut strudel roll into fourths and use a
   spatula to transfer to baking sheet. Repeat with
   remaining filo and filling. Brush tops of strudels with
   oil and bake at 400° until browned. This strudel is
   best served warm.

Makes 12 servings

APPLESAUCE SPICE CAKE

A lactose and sweetening free cake.

1) In a bowl soak **2 c. dried apples** in ½ **c. apple juice.** Preheat oven to 350°. Oil two 9″ round cake pans and line bottoms with waxed paper. Chop ¾ **c. walnuts** and set aside. Measure out ½ **c. raisins** and set aside.

2) In a food processor combine **3**½ **c. whole wheat pastry flour,** ½ **c. soy milk flour, 4 t. baking powder, 1 t. baking soda,** ¾ **t. salt,** and turn machine on to thoroughly mix. Turn out into a large bowl.

3) Use a potato peeler to remove just the outside peel from **1**½ **oranges.** Add peel and **1 c. pitted dates,** packed, to processor and pulverize, stopping machine to scrape down sides. Repeat until dates and peel are as fine as possible. Now add to processor **2 eggs, 3 c. apple sauce** (either homemade or purchased, but without any added sweetening), and puree again. Next add **2 t. cinnamon, 1 t. allspice, 1 t. nutmeg,** ½ **t. cardamom,** ½ **c. carob, 1 Tb. coffee substitute** (such as Cafix, Pero or Bambu). Finally add ⅔ **c. salad oil.** Mix, scrape down, and mix once more.

4) Drain soaked apple slices, and line the bottoms of the cake pans with them. Turn batter from processor into dry mix in bowl, and add walnuts and raisins. Fold all together gently but thoroughly. Turn into prepared pans and bake 45 minutes.

5) Cool on racks. Turn out and remove waxed paper. Chill. This cake tastes best when quite cold. If you like, serve with **Tofu Vanilla Creme** (see recipe index).

Makes two 9″ cakes

But in all the eight years I have lived here, it has not yet become a quiet life. It is life lived at a high pitch. One of the facts about solitude is that one becomes as alert as an animal to every change of mood in the skies, and to every sound. The thud of the first apple falling never fails to startle the wits out of me; there has been no sound like it for a year.

Plant Dreaming Deep
May Sarton; W.W. Norton

GINGERED PEAR ROLL

This delicate, elegant cake has a little honey to sweeten it and no milk products.

1) Start filling: Peel, core and dice **3½-4 lb.** (about 9) firm **Bosc pears.** Put in a pot with **1½ c. apple juice, 1 t. dried ginger, ¼ t. cloves, ¼ t. cinnamon,** and **juice** of ½ **lemon** with **peel** added. Cover and simmer ½ hour or until pears are tender.

2) Make cake: Place **6 eggs** (in their shells) in a bowl of hot water to warm them. Meanwhile, butter a jelly roll pan and line with waxed paper. Squeeze juice from **2 oranges** or enough to make ½ **c. juice.** Set aside.

3) If you have a food processor, separate eggs so that whites go into a mixer and yolks into processor. Or just put yolks into a bowl. In another bowl whisk or sift together **1⅓ c. unbleached white flour** and **¼ t. salt.** Then whisk yolks (or run machine) to beat them thick and light. Add ½ **c. honey** and reserved orange juice to yolks and mix well.

4) Add **1 t. cream of tartar** to whites and beat to soft peak stage. Add **2 Tb. honey** and beat to stiff peaks.

5) Fold yolk mix and flour together. Fold in whites
    gently but thoroughly. Carefully spread batter in
    prepared jelly roll pan. Place in 325° oven and bake
    until cake is light brown and springs back when you
    touch it in the middle. Watch carefully.

6) Have ready a dish towel larger than the cake pan.
    Sift **carob powder** sparingly over it. Run a knife
    around rim of cake, then turn out onto towel. Pull off
    waxed paper in strips. Roll up cake in cloth. Gently
    lift onto rack to cool.

7) Sprinkle **3 Tb. agar-agar flakes** over **2 Tb.
    apple juice** in a cup. Use a potato masher to
    somewhat crush the cooled pears. Add agar-agar to
    pears and simmer 5-10 minutes. If mixture does not
    seem thick enough, add **2½ Tb. arrowroot** or
    cornstarch stirred into **4 Tb. cold apple juice**
    and bring to boil again. Taste. If pears were ripe,
    filling may need **1 Tb. lemon juice.** If they were
    unripe, filling may need **1½ Tb. maple syrup.**

8) Chill filling until thickened and set. Carefully unroll
    cake, spread with pear mixture, and reroll. Chill. If
    you like, serve with **Tofu Vanilla Creme** (see
    recipe index).

                                                          Serves 10

PEAR CUSTARD PIE

1) Prepare **4-5 Bosc pears** as for **Gingered Pear Roll** (see preceding recipe), halving amounts of juice and spices.

2) Roll out a **Pie Crust** (see recipe index) and bake at 400° about 8 minutes, using foil and beans to hold crust flat while baking. Remove foil and beans. Remove crust from oven.

3) Make a custard by beating **2 eggs** in a bowl with a whisk. Add ¼ **c. flour** and continue beating. Add **2 Tb. maple syrup,** ¼ c. of the **pear cooking liquid,** and ¼ **c. heavy cream.** Beat well. Finally, flavor with one of the following: **2½ Tb. plum wine, 2 Tb. cognac,** or ¾ **t. vanilla extract,** as you prefer.

3) Slice pears and arrange them in pie crust. Pour custard over. Sprinkle with **1½ Tb. currants** and bake at 375° until puffed and browned, about 20 minutes. This pie is best served warm.

Let none speak sadly of October,
I, Elsa, from the peak of years,
Say this: I have loved all seasons.

"From the Peak of Years"
Sapphic Songs
Elsa Gidlow; Druid Heights Books

PIE CRUST

It is convenient to have pie crust dough waiting in the refrigerator to be used when you want to make a pie. Wrapped in foil, pie crust will keep 2 weeks refrigerated. So double, triple or quadruple this recipe to have a supply.

1) For each single crust pie shell (with scraps left over), mix together **2 c. flour** and ½ **t. salt.** Cut **1 stick sweet butter** into small bits and place in bowl with flour. Also add **3 Tb. vegetable shortening.** Use the flat beater of a Kitchenaid mixer, a pastry blender, or fingertips to cut fat and flour together until mixture looks like flakes of oatmeal.

2) Add ⅓ **c.** very cold **water.** Mix thoroughly but as briefly as possible. This may be accomplished best by using the heel of your hand to very briefly knead the dough on a floured board.

3) Wrap in foil and chill 2 hours before rolling out dough.

4) Roll out pie crust on a well floured counter or board. Roll crust as thinly as possible. Place in pie pan by first folding dough in half and then gently lifting it into the pie pan. We like removable bottomed quiche pans. Since pie crust will shrink in baking, be sure not to stretch it. If recipe calls for unbaked pie shell, refrigerate crust until ready to use; otherwise preheat oven to 400°. Prick shell at juncture of rim and bottom with a fork. Line shell with aluminum foil and something to weigh foil down, like lentils or beans.

5) Bake about 5 minutes. Carefully remove foil and beans, and add whatever filling needs cooking. Or for a fully baked shell, turn oven down to 375° after removing the foil and bake another 5-10 minutes until evenly browned and done.

6) Scraps of crust can be rolled in **cinnamon-sugar,** cut with a pastry wheel into strips, the strips then twisted and placed on a cookie sheet. Bake at 375° for a tasty cookie.

but there is something else: the faith
of those despised and endangered

that they are not merely the sum
of damages done to them:

have kept beyond violence the knowledge
arranged in patterns like kente-cloth

unexpected as in batik
recurrent as bitter herbs and unleavened bread

of being a connective link
in a long, continuous way

of ordering hunger, weather, death, desire
and the nearness of chaos.

Sources
Adrienne Rich; The Heyeck Press

PEARS POACHED
IN HONEY & RED WINE

A dairy free dessert.

1) Prepare **Almond Oat Cakes** (see following recipe), if desired, to serve with pears.

2) In a saucepan combine **1 c. red wine, 1 Tb. lemon juice, 2 Tb. honey, ¼ t. cinnamon,** and bring to a boil. Turn off heat while preparing pears.

3) Peel, halve, stem, and core **3 large Bosc pears.**

4) Add pears to wine mixture, cover pot, reduce heat to simmer and poach 8-10 minutes. Drain pears into a serving dish. Reduce poaching liquid until syrupy. Pour over pears and chill.

5) To serve, place a pear half on an oat cake and slice, keeping the shape of the pear. Spoon some cooking liquid over and top with **Tofu Vanilla Creme** (see recipe index).

Serves 6

ALMOND OAT CAKES

Delicious under cooked pears or as a cookie.

1) Heat oven to 350°. Lightly oil cookie sheet.

2) Use a food processor to coarsely chop ¾ **c.
   almonds.** Add **3 Tb. oil,** ¼ **c. maple syrup,** ¾
   t. vanilla extract, pinch salt, ¼ **t. cinnamon,**
   ¼ **t. almond extract,** and ⅔ **c. rolled oats.**
   Turn machine on. Add **1½-2 Tb. water** or just
   enough to moisten. Scrape down and mix again.

3) Use a spoon to pat out 10 cookie rounds onto baking
   sheet. Bake until light brown, about 25 minutes. Use
   metal spatula to immediately scrape cookies from
   baking sheet.

10 cookies

*I am scrupulously accurate. I keep track
of all distinctions. Between past and present.
Pain and pleasure.
Living and surviving. Resistance and capitulation.
Will and circumstances. Between life
and death. Yes. I am scrupulously
accurate. I have become a keeper of accounts.*

"Bashert" (Yiddish): inevitable, (pre)destined.
Keeper of Accounts
Irena Klepfisz; Sinister Wisdom

CRANBERRY TOFU MOUSSE

A dairy free dessert.

1) Pour **2 c. apple raspberry juice** into a pot and sprinkle with **2 Tb. agar-agar flakes.** (Agar-agar is a seaweed that works much like gelatin, which is, of course, made from animals.) Let stand a few minutes to soften agar-agar flakes, then bring to a simmer, adding ½ **lb. tofu.** Let simmer 5-10 minutes.

2) Meanwhile, pulverize ¾ **c. nuts** in a food processor. (Use walnuts, almonds, filberts or a combination of these. Sometimes we make up part of the measure with coconut. The nuts provide richness and are the base of this dairy free dessert.) Pulverize as finely as possible. Now, very gradually, begin to add ¾ **c. cooking oil.** Using tongs, lift tofu out of simmering juice. Add pieces of tofu alternately with the oil, proceeding very slowly. Mixture should become thick like mayonnaise. Scrape down. Sweeten with ⅓ **c. maple syrup,** add ¾ **t. salt, 1 t. lemon juice,** and **1 t. vanilla extract.** Finally, add simmered fruit juice and agar-agar. If you think the mousse still seems grainy, and you have a good blender, you may want to further puree mixture in blender.

3) Use a piece of absorbent paper dipped in **oil** to lightly grease 6 custard cups or tea cups. Pour mousse into them and chill.

4) Turn **2 c. cranberries** into a pot with ¼ **c. maple syrup** and ¾ **c. water.** Cook, covered, until the cranberries pop. Cool and chill. If sauce seems too thick, thin with **apple raspberry juice** or **water.**

5) To serve, run a knife around the sides of each custard cup and turn mousse out onto plate. Top with cranberry sauce.

Serves 6

For need can blossom into all the compensations it requires. To crave and to have are as like as a thing and its shadow. For when does a berry break upon the tongue as sweetly as when one longs to taste it, and when is the taste refracted into so many hues and savors of ripeness and earth, and when do our senses know anything so utterly as when we lack it? And here again is a foreshadowing — the world will be made whole. For to wish for a hand on one's hair is all but to feel it. So whatever we may lose, very craving gives it back to us again. Though we dream and hardly know it, longing, like an angel, fosters us, smooths our hair, and brings us wild strawberries.

Housekeeping
Marilynne Robinson; Bantam Books

CHAPTER 2   WINTER

~~~~~~~~~~~~~~~~~~~~~~~~~~~~~~~~~~~~~

DESSERTS

Man corrupt everything, say Shug. He on your box of grits, in your head, and all over the radio. He try to make you think he everywhere. Soon as you think he everywhere, you think he God. But he ain't. Whenever you trying to pray, and man plop himself on the other end of it, tell him to git lost, say Shug. Conjure up flowers, wind, water, a big rock.
But this hard work, let me tell you. He been there so long, he don't want to budge. He threaten lightening, floods and earthquakes. Us fight. I hardly pray at all. Everytime I conjure up a rock, I throw it.

The Color Purple
Alice Walker; Washington Square Press

TEMPEH & MUSHROOMS IN PATTY SHELLS

This recipe makes a rich, delicious filling for baked patty shells, small individual pie shells, or can be a "savory" to go over toast points. It is best served in small portions as a first course before a party meal, such as New Year's Eve. You will need **Miso Gravy** (see recipe index) for this dish.

1) Cut **1 cake tempeh** (8 oz.) horizontally in half, then vertically into thirds, and finally into thinnest possible matchstick pieces. Finely dice **1 large onion** and thinly slice enough **mushrooms** to measure **3½ c.**

2) Heat **3 Tb. oil** in a frying pan. Saute tempeh and vegetables over high heat, stirring constantly, until tempeh begins to brown. Add ⅔ **t. ground coriander** and **1 clove** crushed **garlic** to the pan, continue stirring, and cook until tempeh is well browned. Now add **2½ Tb. flour,** stir together thoroughly, and cook over low heat a few minutes.

3) Add ½ **c. heavy cream,** ⅓ **c. dry sherry,** ⅔ **c. miso gravy,** ⅔ **c. water, 2 t. lemon juice, 1 t. salt,** and freshly ground **pepper.** Bring to simmer, scraping up crispy burnt pieces, and taste to correct seasoning. Finely chop about ½ **c. straight leaf parsley** and fold in. Set aside tempeh mixture to reheat before serving.

4) To make pie crust patty shells, you can use 2 muffin tins, upside down. Preheat oven to 375° and roll out **Pie Crust** (see recipe index). Use a pastry wheel or small knife to cut rough square shapes, one each, to fit over the bottom of each muffin cup. Gently pleat the crust around the cups and prick with a fork. Bake until light brown. When done, carefully lift each shell off pan while warm. Keep at room temperature until ready to serve.

5) Reheat tempeh mixture and spoon into patty shells. Top with a **sprig** of **parsley** and serve.

Serves 10-12 appetizers

Whether the chauvinist mind expresses itself through racist propaganda or through pornography, its delusions are not innocent. For the mind which believes in a delusion must ultimately face reality. And because the chauvinist desperately needs to believe in his delusion, when he is faced with the real nature of the world, he must act. He must force the world to resemble his delusion.

Pornography and Silence
Susan Griffin; Harper and Row

THREE SISTERS SOUP

Made of corn, beans, and squash, this rich and satisfying soup uses the native vegetables particular to North America. This recipe is adapted from Beth Brant of the Mohawk Nation. She serves the soup with fry bread and cabbage salad.

1) Soak ½ **lb. red beans,** such as **cranberry or pinto,** overnight in **water** to cover. Or bring beans to a boil, turn off heat and let sit 1 hour, covered, until ready to proceed.

2) To make the stock, measure **2½ qt. water** (preferably from cooking potatoes) into a large soup kettle. Add **1 large onion,** unpeeled, 1 scraped **carrot, 2-3 outside stalks** and **leaves** of **celery,** 1 scraped **parsnip,** and a **few sprigs** of **dill.** Bring to a boil. For added flavor you may add, if available, a **few bayberry leaves** or **1 dried ancho chili,** depending on whether you are from the Northeast or Southwest. Turn heat down to simmer and cook until vegetables are soft, about 1 hour.

3) Chop **1 onion** and **1 whole head celery.** Mince **2-3 cloves garlic.** Saute vegetables in **2 Tb. oil,** preferably in another soup kettle, until they begin to brown, stirring often.

4) Turn contents of stock pot into a colander over the second pot or a large bowl. Press down on vegetables to extract flavor and then discard.

5) Add the soup stock to the sauteed vegetables. Stir in
   ½ **lb. hominy** (lyed dry corn, available in Hispanic
   markets. Do not use canned hominy). Simmer about 30
   minutes. You will probably need to add **1 qt. water.**

6) Add drained beans and simmer 45 minutes longer.
   Peel ½ **large butternut squash,** and cut into wedge-
   shaped slices. Add to soup with **1 Tb. salt,** and
   simmer until squash is tender.

Serves 8-10

The pathway to the garden
has all but disappeared;
onion sets, like angry fists
have pushed themselves
through the frozen soil

sad pumpkin hearts
have split themselves in two
enraged at being left behind
their vines
stiff and dry as snake skin
tangle in the molding leaves

stalks of corn lean together
like old women
pausing to mourn the scowl
of cold november winds.

"Winter Garden"
Denise Helene Panek
Bearing Witness: Sobreviviendo
Calyx, Vol. 8, No. 2

BEER SOUP WITH SPAETZLE

1) Make soup: Use slicer blade of food processor or a French chef's knife to slice **4 large Spanish onions.** Turn into a soup kettle with **6 Tb. sweet butter** and **1 Tb. +1 t. caraway seeds.** Turn heat to moderately high and cover pot. Stew onions, stirring occasionally, for about 10 minutes. Remove cover and add **1 c. celery stalks** with **leaves,** chopped, and saute mixture with cover off, stirring, about 30 minutes. Add ¼ **c. flour** and stir thoroughly into mixture.

2) Add **2 bottles** warm **light beer** and **6-8 c. water.** Bring to a boil. Add **2 cloves** crushed **garlic, 1¼ t. dried thyme, 1½ Tb. salt, 2½ Tb. shoyu, 2 bay leaves, 2½ Tb. vinegar,** and **1 Tb. miso** (optional). Simmer about 20 minutes.

3) Make **Spaetzle:** Use a mixer (with a flat beater if available) to thoroughly blend **1¾ c. flour, 3 eggs,** ½ **t. salt,** and ¼ **c. water.** Add a **grating** of **nutmeg** and of **pepper.** Beat this soft noodle dough for at least 10 minutes, when you should hear it "slapping".

4) To cook spaetzle, you can use a colander, if you have one with relatively large holes, or a spaetzle device, which holds the batter while sliding over a sieve-shaped plate. Either utensil should be positioned over a pot of simmering water, then the batter can be forced through. After the spaetzle have cooked about 5 minutes, drain in a colander and rinse in cold water.

5) Use a frying pan and **3 Tb. sweet butter,** heated
   very hot, to lightly brown the drained spaetzle.
   Finally, turn the fried spaetzle into a shallow pan and
   bake 10 minutes at 350°.

6) To serve, place warm spaetzle in soup bowls and ladle
   soup over. Chop **1 bunch parsley** as a garnish. Grated
   cheddar cheese is also a nice accompaniment.

Serves 8-10

*But what are you gonna do when your mom's so
miserable and you love her so much that you're
frustrated with bein helpless?
My idea is crawlin through the umbilical cord. Just
close your eyes and pulse your way back to only her . . .
My mom and me position the sieve between our legs
and pick out the bad pinto beans while all the time
she's hummin some songs she don't even know the
words to. Then we cook up a good soup that's gonna
last real long cause we ain't gonna share it with no
men. When at least our stomachs' full and we're not
quite so lonesome, I got to go. But I keep crawlin back
and forth in that umbilical tube, for refills of the soup,
which keeps the tube warm in case she ever does
decide to start again, through me.*

Hurtin & Healin & Talkin It Over
Arny Christine Straayer; Metis Press

PARSNIP & BARLEY STEW

1) Peel and slice 1 package **parsnips,** about **1 lb.** Cut **1 medium onion** into quarters and slice. Put into soup pot, add **2 Tb. oil,** and saute vegetables with ¼ **t. ground cloves** and ½ **t. dried thyme** until golden brown. Add ¼ **c. flour** and stir well with wooden spoon. Add **3 c. water** and **1 medium potato,** peeled, quartered and sliced. Cover and simmer 30 minutes.

2) Separately cook ⅓ **c. pearl barley** in **2 c. water** until done, about 45 minutes.

3) Turn barley plus cooking liquid into soup and season with freshley grated **nutmeg,** 1½ **Tb. shoyu,** 1½ **Tb. lemon juice,** and **2 t. salt.** Add **3 c. milk** and bring to simmer. Top finished soup with chopped **straight leaf parsley** and freshly ground **pepper.**

Serves 6

Water. Spirits. Trees. Spirits. Stones. Spirits. They knew she moved among them. The water saw her with its shining eye. The stones felt her presence. The trees heard her passing. She was forever bound to the great communion of spirits, of which her own was a part.

The Horse Goddess
Morgan Llywelyn; Pocket Books

MARINATED TOFU SALAD

1) Place **1½ lb. tofu** in a pot, cover with **water,** and bring to a boil. Simmer 5 minutes. Turn off heat and let rest another 5 minutes. Drain cakes of tofu; place between sheets of paper toweling and weight to firm up cakes and remove water. Three sturdy plastic trays make a good weight. Leave about 15 minutes.

2) Make marinade: Combine **1 c. salad oil,** ¼ c. **Chinese sesame oil, 2 Tb. lemon juice,** ¼ **c. shoyu,** and **2 Tb. rice wine vinegar.** Whisk well.

3) Cut tofu in half horizontally, then diagonally to form thin triangles about ¼"-½" thick. Lay in a shallow container and spoon some of marinade over. Cover, chill.

4) To serve, shred **1 head Chinese cabbage,** using a large knife. Arrange on plates. Top with tofu triangles. Center with shredded **carrots,** chopped **scallions,** and shredded **daikon** if available. Dress salads with marinade and top with **gomahsio** (see recipe index).

Serve 4-6

MUSHROOM WALNUT PATE

Our intent was to develop a recipe for a dairy-free spread
for bread. The resulting pate is better flavored, we think,
than the best liver pates. We serve it as a salad, though it
could be made of softer consistency for a dip, can be
frozen and defrosted with no change in consistency, and
of course, is delightful spread on bread — especially rye,
fresh out of the oven. The recipe which follows is tricky
and somewhat time consuming. A good quality food
processor is a necessity.

1) In a small coffee mill pulverize **⅓ c. sunflower
   seeds, 2 Tb. sesame seeds,** and if available,
   2 Tb. chia seeds. These seeds are the recipe base
   and must be very finely ground. Use a processor if you
   don't have a mill. Turn seeds into a bowl and set
   aside.

2) Make **Mushroom-Shallot Duxelles:** Coarsely cut
   ½ lb. mushrooms (about 2½ c.) that are clean and
   dry into a food processor. Add about **3 Tb.
   shallots,** peeled and cut up, and chop finely by
   turning machine on and off. Traditionally, duxelles are
   now turned into a clean dish towel over a small bowl,
   and by twisting the towel slowly, the juice is extracted.
   Reserve this liquid. Then heat **2 Tb. oil** in a frying pan
   and when hot, turn duxelles into pan and saute over
   high heat, stirring, until mushroom-shallot mix is
   browned and separated. You can also just turn the
   mixture into the hot frying pan without extracting the
   juice. You should expect to spend more time frying as
   a result. Season duxelles with **salt** and freshly ground
   pepper and set aside.

3) Turn the ground seeds into the unwashed processor and add ½ c. **walnuts, 1 small clove garlic,** peeled, ½ t. **dried oregano,** and ½ t. **dried tarragon.** Have ready in one cup, ⅓ c. **olive oil** and ⅓ c. **cooking oil.** Squeeze **2 Tb. lemon juice.** You will also need ¼ **lb. tofu** (about ½ a cake), shoyu, mustard, and most of all, patience!

4) Turn processor on and very slowly begin to add oil, until the mixture becomes a very stiff paste. This should be much slower than for making mayonnaise. Alternately add pieces of tofu, some lemon juice, and the oil as the machine runs, stretching oil addition to take about 10 minutes. If mixture becomes so stiff as to turn machine off, then pate is proceeding properly. Add a little lemon juice to start it up again. Do not use all the lemon juice, taste to see whether you want 1½-2 Tb. of it. You will need ⅔ t. **prepared mustard** and **1½-2 Tb. shoyu** as final seasoning. If pate seems too stiff, add a little of the reserved **mushroom juice** or **water.** Remaining mushroom juice may be saved for soups. If oil was added too quickly, you may find signs of separation as machine works. Turn machine off, pour excess oil back into cup measure, and turn machine on. After a minute or two, begin dribbling oil in again until it is properly incorporated.

5) In a bowl fold together the duxelles and contents of processor. Chill.

6) We serve the pate in the center of a ½" **thick green pepper ring** on a bed of **Boston lettuce,** surrounded by **cucumber slices** and **celery hearts.** The salad is lightly sprinkled with **paprika** and drizzled with **vinaigrette.** Finally, the pate is topped with a **fluted raw mushroom.**

Yields 2 cups

One of the greatest gifts of Black feminism to ourselves has been to make it a little easier simply to be Black and female. A Black feminist analysis has enabled us to understand that we are not hated and abused because there is something wrong with us, but because our status and treatment is absolutely prescribed by the racist, misogynistic system under which we live . . . Until Black feminism, very few people besides Black women actually cared about or took seriously the demoralization of being female and colored and poor and hated.

Home Girls: A Black Feminist Anthology
Barbara Smith; Introduction
Ed. Barbara Smith;
Kitchen Table: Women of Color Press

TEMPEH POT PIE

1) First prepare **Miso Gravy** (see recipe index).

2) In a frying pan stew **2 cakes tempeh** (16 oz.) in ½ c.
   red wine, ¼ c. **shoyu**, ½ c. **water**, **2 cloves**
   crushed **garlic**, ¼ t. **coriander**, and ½ t. **ground
   ginger** (dried) for 5-10 minutes. Drain tempeh,
   reserving broth. Cut into diamond shapes and fry in
   2 Tb. oil until lightly browned. Set aside.

3) In a large soup pot brown **1½ c. carrots** and **1½ c.
   celery**, cut into diagonal wedge shapes. Add **1½ c.
   pearl onions**, peeled, and **2 c. fresh whole
   mushrooms**. When lightly browned, add ½ t.
   thyme, ¼ t. **sage**, 2 c. peeled diced **potatoes,
   1½ c. miso gravy**, **1½ c. water**, and **2 bay leaves**.
   Simmer until vegetables are done, about 30 minutes. If
   you like, separately boil **3 c.** diced peeled **rutabaga**
   in **water** halfway to cover. They will take almost 1
   hour to cook.

4) Prepare **Buttermilk Biscuits:** Use a whisk to stir
   together **2⅓ c. flour, 1½ Tb. baking powder,**
   ¾ t. **baking soda**, ¾ t. **salt.** Use a pastry blender
   or 2 knives to cut in ⅔ **stick butter** until mixture
   looks like oatmeal flakes. Stir in **1 c. buttermilk.**
   Pat out on floured board, cut into rounds, prick tops
   with fork and bake at 450° until browned, about 10
   minutes.

5) Just before serving, combine tempeh with vegetables
   and gravy, rutabagas, **2 Tb.** chopped **parsley,** and
   ¼ c. peas. Turn into a casserole and add more
   gravy or **vegetable cooking water** to thin
   adequately. Top with biscuits and reheat in oven.

Serves 6-8

My heart shudders under red wool,
and there is not enough sun to warm me,
Artemis of the animals, loose
in the red zone, on the brink
of the twenty-first century,
at the close of a millenium of death:

blue whale, Polish Jew, tiger, witch, lion
sperm whale, whooping crane, black South African,
elk, mountain goat, the women of every country,
slugs in the garden, Indians in Chile, Guatemala,
El Salvador, Tacoma, Detroit, crows in the crops,
rattlesnake, migrant pickers in Hood River, Yakima,
bald eagle, dolphin, timber wolf, the inhabitants
of any ghetto, refugee or concentration camp, seal,
sea otter, fox, coyote,
the genes of the unborn
flooded with purple light
the eye refuses to see.

Notes From the Red Zone
Christina V. Pacosz; Seal Press

MISO GRAVY

This version of our Miso Gravy makes use of Guinness Stout instead of plain beer. The substitution was suggested by Michael Russo. Of course, you may use any beer you have on hand, but the Guinness gives the gravy a deeper, more interesting flavor.

1) Finely chop **2 Tb. onions** and saute in a saucepan with **1 stick sweet butter** (or ½ **c. vegetable oil**) along with **2 cloves** crushed **garlic, 6** minced **mushrooms,** ½ **t. dried thyme,** and ½ **t. dried basil.** Cook over medium heat, stirring frequently, until well browned.

2) Add ½ **c. unbleached white flour.** Cook several minutes, stirring constantly. Add **6 oz. Guinness Stout** and enough **water** to make gravy (vegetable cooking water is best if you have some available). Add **3 Tb. red or brown miso, 1 Tb. tomato paste, 2 Tb. dry sherry,** and **1 Tb. shoyu.**

3) Simmer slowly for 30 minutes. Correct seasoning.

Yields over 1 qt. of gravy

MUSHROOM STROGANOFF

This easy stroganoff from animal rights' activist, Esther Meckler, has exceptionally fine flavor.

1) Slice **1½ lb. large mushrooms.** Slice **1 large Spanish onion.** Turn into frying pan with **2 cloves** crushed **garlic** and **2 Tb. oil.** Fry over highest heat. Add **1 Tb.** good quality **Hungarian paprika** and **1 t. thyme.** Cook, stirring well, until mushrooms are well browned.

2) Add ½ c. **dry sherry, 1 Tb. tomato paste, 2 bay leaves,** ¼ c. **shoyu, 4 oz. cream cheese,** and **1 c. sour cream.** Bring to a simmer and finish seasoning with a little freshly ground **black pepper, 1 Tb. lemon juice,** and a **splash** of **brandy.** If stroganoff is too thick, thin with **water.**

3) Serve over cooked **egg noodles** with **poppy seeds** and freshly chopped **straight leaf parsley.**

Serves 4

CREPES SOUFFLES WITH SHALLOT WINE HOLLANDAISE

An elaborate party dish we serve at New Years, together with an endive salad and a winter fruit bowl of pineapple, oranges, kiwi, pears, and kumquat.

1) Stew **1 lb. tofu** in ⅓ **c. white wine,** ¼ **c. shoyu,** and **1 bay leaf** for 5 minutes. Drain tofu and place on absorbent paper. Reserve liquid. Weight tofu with 2 trays. Separately stew ¼ **lb. mushrooms,** quartered, in ⅓ **c. water.** And in a third small pot make a broth by cooking a **3" piece** of **kombu** in ⅔ **c. water** about 10 minutes. Set aside.

2) Peel and shred **1 large parsnip.** Set aside.

3) To make souffle base, melt **3 Tb. sweet butter** in a saucepan. Add ⅓ **t. dried tarragon, pinch thyme,** ½ **t. dried mustard,** and ¼ **c. flour.** Cook together, stirring, several minutes. Add reserved liquids from drained tofu, mushrooms, and kombu. Stirring well, bring to a boil. Add ¼ **c. milk, 1 t. lemon juice,** and remove from heat. Sauce will be stiff. Whisk in ¼ **c. heavy cream,** ¼ **c. dry sherry,** and a **drop** or **two** of **Tabasco.** Separate **4 eggs,** reserving whites. Whisk yolks into souffle base when it is cool enough not to curdle them.

4) Season souffle base with **salt** and **pepper** to taste, **pinch cardamom, 1 Tb. fresh parsley,** chopped fine, **1 Tb. catsup,** and ¾ **c. Swiss cheese,** grated. Mince kombu and add. Cut tofu into scallop shaped pieces. Fold tofu, mushrooms and parsnip into sauce. Correct seasoning and refrigerate.

5) To make crepe batter, melt **4 Tb. sweet butter.**
Put the following ingredients into a blender: ¾ **c.
milk, ¾ c. cold water, 4 eggs, 3 yolks** (reserve
whites), **1½ c. unbleached white flour, ½ t.
salt,** and blend. Scrape down sides, add melted
butter, and blend again. Refrigerate batter in blender
pitcher for an hour or more.

6) You will need well seasoned crepe pans, preferably 3,
to make crepes. To season pans, heat over a low
flame with a little oil for 15 minutes. Wipe out oil.
Never wash pans, wipe out with oily paper, and don't
use for any other purpose than for crepes. Mix crepe
batter again just before using. Heat pans, wipe with
oiled absorbent paper, and make crepes by pouring a
little batter into the pan, tipping quickly around, and
pouring back excess if any. When edges brown and
curl, use spatula to lift crepe and briefly cook on other
side. Repeat, stacking crepes on a plate as they are
done. Cover with plastic wrap and refrigerate. You will
have more crepes than you will need for this recipe.

7) Prepare **Shallot Wine Hollandaise:** Saute **1 Tb.
shallots,** minced, in **2 Tb. butter** until soft. Add
½ **c. white wine** and reduce (boil down) to ¼ c.
Remove from heat and cool a few minutes, than whisk
in **3 egg yolks.** Melt **12 Tb. sweet butter** in a
separate pot. Whisk yolk and wine mixture over low
heat until it thickens slightly, then add melted butter
slowly, until sauce thickens like a hollandaise.
Remove from heat; add **salt** and **pepper** to taste,
plus a **few drops** of **lemon juice.** Cover and leave
near the stove where it will stay warm, but not so
close to heat that it will curdle.

8) When ready to serve, heat oven to 400°. Stiffly beat
   ½ c. of the reserved **egg whites** with **pinch** of **salt**
   until stiff but not dry. Fold in the tofu-parsnip souffle
   base. Use a spoon to place a dollop on each crepe,
   then fold in half, and then into quarters. Place quickly
   on a buttered baking sheet. Crepes will puff, so don't
   over fill them. Place in oven and reduce heat to 375°.
   Bake until puffed and browned, about 10 minutes.

9) Place 2-3 crepes on each plate. Spoon Wine Shallot
   Hollandaise over the crepes. Steamed **broccoli** is a
   nice accompaniment.

Serves 12

Monika said, "Whenever I think of men on the moon
I get a picture in my head. Of bugs beating
senselessly against a light bulb. Buzz. Buzz. And then
they burn up."
"Do you think they'll die there then?" I asked.
"Perhaps. The moon is a woman, you know, in every
language but German. Maybe she'll grow angry
when they try to land, maybe she'll burn them up with
her light."

Walking on the Moon
Barbara Wilson; Seal Press

WINTER THALI

Indian cuisine offers a wealth of interesting food to vegetarians. We make an elaborate Winter Thali which includes deep fried vegetable dumplings in a chick pea flour batter (**Pakora**) served with **Tamarind** and **Cilantro Chutneys.** Purchased **Pappadums** are also fried as appetizers. The main platter (or thali) has **Basmati Rice** in the center with small cups surrounding it. The cups (or katoori) contain mixed root vegetables (**Korma**), mustard green and spinach **Saag**, a lentil gravy called **Dahl** to pour over the rice, and a salad of cucumber and yoghurt (**Raita**). We buy **Hot Lime Pickle** (the preferred brand is Bedeker) at a local Indian store, and we serve **Paratha** (layered, unleavened bread) on the side. Three or four cooks can make the whole thali as a party meal. Some ingredients will require access to an Indian market.

And so Kai Talvela followed the Moon to her cave beneath the ocean. Time is different there than it is beneath the light of the sun, and it seemed to her that no time passed at all. She slept by day, and rose at night to ride with the Moon across the dark sky's face, to race the wolves across the plains and watch the dolphins playing in the burnished sea.

"The Woman Who Loved The Moon"
Elizabeth A. Lynn
Lesbian Fiction
Ed: Elly Bulkin; Persephone Press

GARAM MASALA

Garam masala is an all purpose blend of spices essential to Indian cooking. Other spices or herbs, suitable for an individual dish or favored by the cook, may be added to the basic blend. Here is the classic combination of spices in proportions we find pleasing. You will have to shop in an Indian market for the ingredients. Try to get true cinnamon, not cassia which is the stiff "stick cinnamon" available in supermarkets.

1) Preheat oven to 200°. Spread following ingredients over the bottom of a large, shallow baking pan; $\frac{1}{3}$ **c. cinnamon pieces, $\frac{1}{2}$ c. whole cloves, $\frac{1}{2}$ c. cumin seeds, $\frac{1}{4}$ c. coriander seeds, $\frac{3}{4}$ c. cardamom pods,** and $\frac{1}{4}$ **c. peppercorns.** Roast for 30 minutes, stirring occasionally. Do not brown spices.

2) Break open cardamom pods, remove the seeds, and discard the pods. This takes patience.

3) Grind all spices together in a blender or electric coffee mill in appropriately sized batches. Store in an airtight container in a cool place.

Yields approximately 2 cups

PAKORA

Deep fried vegetable dumplings in a chick pea flour
batter. Serve with **Cilantro** and **Tamarind
Chutneys.**

1) In a small bowl whisk together **1 c. besan**
   (chick pea flour, available at Indian markets), **1 t.
   cumin, 1 t. cayenne pepper, ½ t. baking soda,**
   and **2 t. salt.** Set aside.

2) Dice **2-3 small** peeled **potatoes** and place in a
   bowl. Slice **1 small onion** and add to potatoes.
   Separate ½ **cauliflower** into flowerets, cut small.
   Add to potatoes and cover vegetables with **cold
   water.** Refrigerate until ready to serve.

3) Heat **3 c. oil** in a wok so that you can deep fry
   pakoras. Use a slotted spoon to lift vegetables out of
   water. Add to dry mix, adding as much of the cold
   water as necessary to make a soft batter. Fold in
   2 Tb. chopped **cilantro.** Use 2 spoons to drop
   batter into hot oil and fry for 3-4 minutes. Drain well
   on absorbent paper. If you like, cut purchased
   pappadums in half and fry them also. They cook in
   seconds.

4) Serve with chutneys (see following recipes).

Serves 8-10

TAMARIND CHUTNEY

1) Soak **4 oz. tamarind seeds** and **pulp** in **1 c. warm water** for about 30 minutes. Break up the seeds and pulp, using your fingers. Separate out all seeds and discard.

2) Mix tamarind pulp with **2 Tb. molasses, 3 Tb. raisins,** ¼ **c.** chopped **dried apples,** ½ **t.** grated **fresh ginger,** and **2. t. salt.** Add **1 t. garam masala** (see recipe index) and **pinch cayenne pepper.** Dilute with **water** as desired. Refrigerate and serve with Indian Thali dinner.

Yields about 2 cups

CILANTRO CHUTNEY

1) Wash and shake dry **2 c. cilantro leaves** (Chinese parsley). Put into a processor with **1 t.** diced **fresh ginger,** ⅓ **c.** chopped **onion,** ½ **small chili pepper,** ⅓ **c. dried unsweetened coconut, 1 t. salt,** and ½ **t. honey.** Process.

2) Add **plain yoghurt** to taste, about ½ **c.** Refrigerate.

Yields about 2½ cups

KORMA

Root vegetables cooked in almond cardamom sauce.
Some of these spices are available only at Indian
markets.

1) In a small pot cover ¼ **c. almonds** with **water** and
   bring to a boil. Drain and slip skins off. Put almonds
   into a food processor with **1" fresh ginger,** peeled;
   1 hot chili, seeded; **1" stick cinnamon** (true
   cinnamon is preferred); **2 Tb. white poppy seeds**
   (this is optional, but don't substitute black poppy
   seeds); **1 Tb. ground coriander; 1 t. whole
   cumin seed; 2 cloves garlic,** peeled; **3 whole
   cloves; and** ¼ **t. ground cardamom seed.**
   Turn machine on to pulverize spices. You will have to
   scrape down the machine and repeat twice.

2) Heat **2 Tb. water** in a small pot and add ¼ **t.
   saffron.** Set aside.

3) If you like, you can add **tofu** to korma. Use a heavy
   plate to weight ½ lb. tofu to make it firmer in texture.

4) Peel and cut into 1" cubes **2 medium large
   potatoes.** Thinly slice **1 large carrot.** Peel and cut
   2 white turnips or ⅓ **rutabaga** into cubes. Scrape
   and slice **3 parsnips.** Chop **2 c. onions.** Put
   potatoes into a bowl and cover with cold water. Set all
   the other vegetables aside.

5) If you are using tofu, dice it. Heat **2 T. oil** in a large frying pan until quite hot. Fry tofu until it's light brown and crispy. Use a slotted spoon to remove to a bowl. Now turn heat down to low and gently toast ½ **c. cashews** in the same pan. Be careful to stir, since they burn easily. When light brown, remove to the same bowl as tofu.

6) Adding more **oil** if necessary, saute chopped onions in the frying pan. While they cook, add the spice mixture from the processor (called a "masala") and cook, stirring, until onions wilt and turn golden. Add carrots, rutabagas and parsnips. Saute a few minutes more. Turn mixture into a pot large enough to hold all the vegetables, being sure to scrape all seasonings into the pot as well. Drain potatoes and add to the pot. Cover and cook over low heat about 10 minutes. Add **2 c. yoghurt,** cover again, and stew mixture another 10-15 minutes. Now add **1 c. water** or as much as needed to make mixture creamy. Add **2 t. salt** and resume cooking until vegetables are tender. Taste to see whether **salt** and **water** are necessary.

7) Chop **2 Tb. cilantro** and fold into korma.

Serves 8

. . . honor thy mother, rejoice the Goddess with the fruits of the earth, do not injure animals.

Ariadne
June Rachuy Brindel; St. Martin's Press

SAAG

1) Thoroughly wash **1 lb. mustard greens.** Bring a pot of **water** to a boil and add greens. Return to boil and cook a few minutes. Drain well. This step minimizes bitterness.

2) Wash **1 lb. spinach.** Slice both spinach and mustard greens thinly. Saag can be made with spinach alone, but this combination is more interesting.

3) Melt ½ **c. sweet butter** in a frying pan and add **1½ t. whole cumin seed, 1 small hot pepper,** seeded and chopped, and **1 large clove garlic,** chopped. Wash your hands well with soap after handling hot pepper. Add **1 t. tumeric** to pan. When butter is hot, begin to add the mustard greens. Fry over high heat, turning frequently. As greens wilt, add more. After a few minutes, begin adding spinach and continue frying and turning until spinach wilts. Add **1½ t. ground cumin** (both whole and ground cumin are necessary to this dish) and **2½ t. ground coriander.** Finally, add about **1 t. salt.** Cover and simmer 10 minutes.

4) Taste saag for salt. Reheat gently before serving as part of an Indian Thali.

Serves 6-8

DAHL

A gravy made of lentils or beans. Masur is made from red lentils; moong from split mung beans, generally available. We also like chana and urad dahl, available at Indian markets. Even supermarket split peas can be used.

1) Soak **1 c. lentils (dahl)** in **water** to cover for about 1 hour. Drain, checking carefully to see there are no stones. Turn into a pot, cover again with fresh **water** and add **1 t. tumeric.** Bring to a boil, cover, and simmer for 1 hour or more, until the dahl is tender. Add **water** as necessary, checking every 10 minutes.

2) To season dahl, chop ½ **onion** and mince **1 clove garlic.** In a small frying pan melt **4 Tb. butter** and begin cooking ½ **t. whole black mustard seeds** until seeds begin to pop. Add onion and garlic, and turn heat off. Finely dice enough **ginger** to yield **1 t.;** add to pan. Chop ¼ of a **hot chili pepper,** and add to pan. Add ¼ **t. ground cumin,** ½ **t. ground coriander,** and the crushed seed of **1 cardamom pod,** if available. A mortar and pestle or a rolling pin work well. Simmer all together about 5 minutes.

3) Add above sauce, called a "tadka", to the dahl with **1½ t. salt.** Simmer another 30 minutes and taste. You may need more salt. Dahl should be a thin gravy to serve over rice, so add **water** as necessary.

Makes 3-4 cups

BASMATI RICE

There is no substitute for the fragrance and flavor of real basmati rice. Available in most health food stores and in Indian markets.

1) Cover **2 c. basmati rice** with **cold water** and pour off chaff which will rise to the surface. Repeat several times until rice is clean.

2) Turn rice into a shallow wide pot or frying pan. Cover with **water.** Bring to a simmer, tightly covered. Cook 10-15 minutes, checking that water is adequate.

Serves 6-8

There is a chronic condition common among freudian women authors, jungian women authors, christian women authors, marxian women authors, new age-ean women authors, et al. That condition, often unmentioned, is mentorship by men. The mental blocks of pseudo-generic women are mentor blocks. Moreover, the mendacity of men-mentors is unmendable, unendable, under the reign of men. It can be mended only when this reign is ended, for women under men's mentorship are minds divided, derided.

Pure Lust
Mary Daly; Beacon Press

RAITA

Cucumber yoghurt salad.

1) Peel and dice **1 small cucumber.** Combine with
   1 quart plain yoghurt in a bowl.

2) In a small pan dry roast **2 Tb. whole cumin
   seeds** until fragrant and slightly browned. Let cool a
   little, then use a mortar and pestle to crush seeds.
   Finely chop **1 small onion** and enough **cilantro**
   (Chinese parsley) to measure ¼ **c.**

3) Season raita with **1½ t. salt,** freshly ground
   pepper, the ground cumin, onion, and cilantro.
   Refrigerate until ready to serve.

Serves 6

*She shook her head slowly. "They are afraid, Tayo.
They feel something happening, they can see something
happening around them, and it scares them. Indians or
Mexicans or whites — most people are afraid of
change. They think that if their children have the same
color of skin, the same color of eyes, that nothing is
changing." She laughed softly. "They are fools. They
blame us, the ones who look different. That way they
don't have to think about what has happened inside
themselves."*

Ceremony
Leslie Marmon Silko; Signet

PARATHA

A layered Indian flat bread.

1) Paratha cannot be made without chapati flour,
   available only in Indian markets. Put **2 c. chapati
   flour** in a food processor. Add **1 c. unbleached
   white flour** and **1 t. salt.** Whirl these dry
   ingredients together. Measure out **3 Tb. oil** and **1 c.
   lukewarm water.** Turn machine on and add oil
   slowly; then add water gradually, adding just enough
   to make a dough which forms into a cohesive ball.
   Continue to run processor for a minute or two to
   knead dough thoroughly. Remove to a bowl, cover
   with a towel, and let rest in a warm place for about
   ½ hour.

2) Pour about ⅓ **c. oil** into a shallow bowl. Remove
   dough to a board sprinkled with chapati flour and
   divide in half. Roll each half into a rope and the divide
   each rope into 8 pieces. Roll each piece into a ball and
   return to bowl, covering again with towel. Remove 1
   ball at a time and use a rolling pin to roll out into a
   circle approximately 5″ in diameter. Using a pastry
   brush, coat lightly with **oil**, fold in half, brush lightly
   again, and fold into quarters. Now gently roll into a
   rounded triangular shape about 6-7″ in diameter. Place
   on a tray sprinkled with chapati flour and repeat
   procedure with remaining dough balls. Place waxed
   paper between layers of parathas so that they will not
   stick together.

3) When all are formed, heat a griddle or cast iron skillet to moderately hot. Depending on the size of your cooking surface, place 1-4 parathas in a single layer on the hot metal. In about 15 seconds they will begin to puff. Use a spatula to flip them over. If the temperature is right, they will not be browned. Brush lightly with **oil** and turn immediately again. Brush the other side with **oil**. The parathas will have been cooked once on each side with no oil and once on each side lightly oiled. Each time they will puff and fall. When done properly, they are flecked light brown. Remove to a plate when done and repeat procedure until entire batch is cooked.

4) Wrap parathas carefully in foil and refrigerate. When ready to serve, they can be reheated one at a time by sprinkling lightly with a few drops of **water**, wrapped airtight in foil, and then heated for 5-10 minutes in a 350° toaster oven. Or you can reheat the entire batch in a similar fashion in a large oven.

Makes 16 parathas

The moon, the sun, the stars
Come through my door
Love sweeps across my wooden floor
And gathers me up in arms so strong
And carries me on a winter song.

"The Moon, The Sun, The Stars"
Laura Wetzler
Touch And Go; *Laura Wetzler Music.*

POLENTA WITH DAIRY FREE "CHEESE" SAUCE & VEGETABLES

The recipe for this unusual sauce is from Susan Foley.

1) Make **Polenta:** Bring **2 c. water** to a boil in large pot with **1 t. salt.** Meanwhile, stir together **1½ c. cornmeal** (preferably fresh ground from a health food store) with **1⅓ c. cold water.** Use a whisk to stir cornmeal and boiling water together. Add **2 Tb. oil,** stir, and cover pot. Lower heat to simmer for about 10 minutes. Uncover, raise heat to moderate and use a wooden spoon to stir cornmeal off and on for 15-20 minutes. Turn out onto a large, round dinner plate to form a thick, cake-like circle. Cool, wrap in plastic, and chill.

2) Make the **"Cheese" Sauce:** In a pot, whisk together **1 c. nutritional yeast** (from the health food store), **⅓ c. whole wheat flour, 3 Tb. arrowroot,** and **1 t. salt.** Measure out **3 c. water,** and add some of it to the dry mix, using a whisk to stir. Turn heat on, and add water gradually, whisking all the while. Add as much water as seems necessary to get a good creamy consistency. Finish by adding **⅓ c. oil.** Use a fork or potato masher to coarsely break up **1 lb. tofu.** Stir into sauce. Cover to keep warm until serving time.

3) Steamed or fried vegetables complete this dish. You can use any you like. For example, slice **2 c. mushrooms,** ½ **small eggplant,** peeled, **1 large onion,** and **1 large red pepper.** Fry in **2-3 Tb. olive oil** with ¼ **t. hot pepper flakes,** ½ **t. basil,** and ½ **t. oregano.** When vegetables begin to brown, add **2 cloves** crushed **garlic,** ⅓ **head broccoli,** divided into flowerettes, and **2-3 c. Swiss chard** or **escarole,** sliced thinly. When vegetables are all tender, season with ¼ **c. shoyu,** cover, and remove from heat. Vegetables may be combined with "cheese" sauce and reheated later or kept separate.

4) To serve, cut the polenta into 6 wedges. Slice each in half horizontally to make pieces thinner. Dip in **flour** and fry in a little **oil** in a very hot frying pan or on a griddle until golden and crispy on each side. Two pieces placed point to point like a butterfly on a plate make a single serving. Top with sauce and vegetables.

Serves 6

We are not the first women to have known what we know, we are not without precedents — despite the frequency with which we and our foremothers are presented as new. We are not inventing our rebellion, but reinventing it.

Women of Ideas
Dale Spender; Ark Paperbacks

TEMPEH IN ORANGE JUICE & RED WINE

Adapted from an Israeli chicken dish, this is an easy and tasty way to do tempeh, from Batya Bauman. She serves the tempeh and accompanying rice with a **Sabra Salad** (see recipe index), but since local tomatoes and cucumbers don't coincide with orange season here, we have listed these recipes in separate chapters.

1) Cut **2 dozen salt cured, wrinkled olives** (called "Greek" in some delicatessens) from their pits. Place olives in a small pot and cover with **1½ c. water.** Simmer 10 minutes. Remove olive pieces and cut coarsely. Reserve olive liquid and olives in separate bowls.

2) Cut **2 cakes tempeh** (1 lb.) into 1" squares or diamonds. On a sheet of waxed paper, shake together **½ c. flour** and **½ t. ground coriander.** Dip tempeh pieces in this seasoned flour.

3) Heat **2 Tb. olive oil** in a frying pan and add tempeh, frying only as many pieces as will fit in one layer at a time. Fry until nicely browned on both sides. Remove to an ovenproof casserole and repeat until all tempeh is done. Turn off heat.

4) Thinly slice **2 red onions.** Squeeze **juice** from 7-8 oranges or enough to measure **2 c. orange juice.** Measure **1 c. dry red wine.** Add onions, juice, wine and olive liquid to frying pan and bring to a boil. Add **2 t. salt, 1½ t. dried thyme,** and freshly ground **pepper** to taste. Pour over tempeh in the casserole. Cover with lid or foil and bake in 350° oven for 1 hour.

5) At same time roast **1 c. raw peanuts** in a separate pan until nicely browned. Remove from oven and set aside to cool.

6) Uncover casserole and sprinkle reserved olives over it. Cover and bake 20 minutes more.

7) Make **Peanut Rice** ("Orez Botnim") to go with tempeh: Saute **2 c. rice** in **2 Tb. olive oil,** adding **½ t. dried ginger, ½ t. ground cinnamon, 1½ t. salt.** When translucent, cover with **3 c. water** and add **1½ Tb. honey.** Cook, covered, 10-15 minutes.

8) Turn roasted peanuts into a dish towel and crush coarsely with a rolling pin.

9) To serve, top rice with crushed peanuts and serve with tempeh. Garnish plates with **orange slices.**

Serves 6

LLAPINGACHOS CON SALSA DE MANI

A traditional Ecuadorian potato and cheese croquette. In this recipe tofu replaces the cheese. From Ricardo Jennings of Tao-Fu, Quito, Ecuador.

1) Toast ½ **lb. unsalted peanuts** in a 400° oven until lightly browned, stirring every few minutes for 10-15 minutes total. Set aside.

2) Wash **6 medium sized potatoes;** cut into large chunks, cover with water in a pot, and boil until just tender. Drain well and set aside.

3) If available, gently heat **1 Tb. annatto seed** (achiote) in **2 Tb. oil** until it is quite yellow. Discard the seeds.

4) Trim **3 scallions** and peel **3 cloves garlic.** Chop the scallions and add with crushed garlic to the annatto colored oil. Saute until golden.

5) Peel potatoes and put into a mixer. Beat well. Add ½ **lb. tofu,** ½ **Tb. salt,** sauteed garlic and scallions, and freshly ground **pepper.** Mix well again. Taste for salt and pepper; correct seasoning. Turn mixture into container and chill.

6) For **Salsa de Mani** (peanut sauce), chop another **3 scallions** and crush another **2 cloves garlic.** Saute in frying pan in **1 Tb. oil** with ⅓ **t. hot pepper flakes,** ½ **t. dried rosemary,** ½ **t. oregano,** and ¾ **t. ground cumin.** Use a blender or food processor to pulverize the peanuts with the sauteed vegetables and seasonings, adding another ¼ **lb. tofu** and **2-3 c. water** as needed. Try to get the sauce as smooth and creamy as possible. Flavor with **2-3 Tb. shoyu** and ½ **Tb. miso.** Mix again and correct seasonings. Add **Tabasco sauce** if not spicy enough for your taste. Turn sauce into a pot and bring to a simmer. Try to get the sauce as smooth and creamy as possible. Flavor with **2-3 Tb. shoyu** and ½ **Tb. miso.** Mix again and correct seasonings. Add **Tabasco sauce** if not spicy enough for your taste. Turn sauce into a pot and bring to a simmer.

7) We like to garnish the Llapingacho plate with cooked beets, so scrape **1 small bunch** of **beets,** barely cover with **water** in a pot and cook until just done, about 20 minutes.

8) When ready to serve, heat a frying pan or griddle until hot. If potato mixture seems soft, shape 3 cakes per person on a **flour** sprinkled sheet of waxed paper. Otherwise, use your hands to shape cakes. Add **oil** to griddle or skillet and fry cakes over high heat until edges look brown and crusted. Use spatula to scrape up each cake, turn over and press down so that finished cakes are about ½"-¾" thick. While second

side browns, cut long vertical slices of **ripe plantain**
to fry alongside potato cakes. Serve Llapingachos with
peanut sauce, plantain slices, shredded **lettuce** and
avocado. Slice beets for the side of the platter and
top potato cakes with minced **scallions.**

Serves 6-8

*Most Latinas, in looking to find some kind of literary
tradition among our women, will usually speak of the
"cuentos" our mothers and grandmothers told us . . .
For the most part, our lives and the lives of the women
before us have never been fully told, except by word of
mouth . . . But we can no longer afford to keep our
tradition oral . . . This way of life that kept our tales re-
told is falling apart; for they have taken the storytellers
and scattered us all over the world . . . for so many
Latinas who can no longer claim our own country, or
even the domain of our own homes — barely holding la
tierra below our feet — we need una literatura that
testifies to our lives, provides acknowledgement of who
we are: an exiled people, a migrant people, mujeres en
lucha.*

"Testimonio"
Cuentos: Stories by Latinas
*Ed: Alma Gómez, Cherríe Moraga, Mariana
Romo-Carmona; Kitchen Table Press*

ENCHILADAS CON SALSA VERDE WITH CHEESE OR TOFU FILLING

Tomatillo Sauce from Mona Jill Vexler.

1) Make Salsa Verde: Wash and remove papery husks from **1½ lb. fresh tomatillos.** These are available in Hispanic markets sporadically in the Northeast and more consistently in the South and West, we presume. Cut tomatillos coarsely and put in a pot with **1 large Spanish onion,** cut up, **2-3 hot peppers** (such as Serranos) seeded, and **3-4 cloves garlic.** Add ½ **c. water,** cover, and stew gently over low heat for about 20 minutes. Tomatillos should yield enough juice so mixture won't burn.

2) Ladle mixture into blender or processor and process briefly in several batches. Don't puree. Turn into a container and season with ½ **c.** finely chopped **cilantro** and **1 t. salt.**

3) Make **Tortillas:** Combine ½ **c. soy flour, 1¾ c. masa harina, 1 t. salt,** and **1 c. water.** It is easy to do this in a food processor, but can also be done by hand. Tortilla dough cannot be over mixed. Soy flour helps keep tortillas flexible. If dough seems damp and sticky, add a little more **masa harina;** if it seems dry, add a few drops more **water.** Divide dough into 15 balls and cover with a cloth. Use a tortilla press and 2 baggies or squares of waxed paper to shape tortillas. Place on a tray separated by sheets of waxed paper until all are pressed.

4) Using a frying pan, grill one tortilla at a time in very little **oil.** Heat frying pan so that it takes about 20 seconds per side to tinge tortillas light brown. Moderate heat is best. Lift tortillas out and stack them on top of each other while the rest are pan-grilled.

5) Divide **1 lb. queso blanco** (available in Hispanic stores) into 15 finger length pieces. Finely chop **1 onion.** Top each tortilla with a piece of cheese, a little onion, and a tablespoon of tomatillo sauce. Roll up and align tortillas side by side in a baking casserole. Cover and refrigerate.

6) For a dairy free dinner, tortillas can be filled with lengths of **tofu.** Sprinkle the tofu lengths with **nutritional yeast** and a little **shoyu,** add the onion and tomatillo sauce, then roll up.

7) Prepare **Refried Beans** and **Spanish Rice** (see following recipes).

8) To serve, bake enchiladas at 350° with a little more salsa verde on top for about 15 minutes. Heat extra sauce to serve alongside. Serve with beans and rice. A thin drizzle of **Spanish Sauce** (see *The Political Palate* recipe index) in a stripe over the salsa verde makes a pretty plate. Add sliced **avocado** as a garnish.

Serves 7

REFRIED BEANS

1) Soak **1½ c. dried kidney** or **pinto beans** overnight. When ready to cook, bring the beans to a boil in sauce pot with **water** to barely cover. If beans cannot be soaked overnight, they can be brought to a boil in water, removed from heat and left covered for one hour. Beans will taste better and be more tender if soaked overnight. Either way, cook until tender, about 45 minutes. Check beans periodically and add **water** if necessary, but keep the amount of liquid to a minimum.

2) Meanwhile, chop **1 large onion.** Fry in ¼ **c. oil** in a large saucepan over medium high heat. Add **1½ Tb. ground dried ancho chilis** (or **1 Tb. chili powder).** Continue frying until onions begin to lightly brown.

3) When beans are very tender, dip them out of pot with a slotted spoon and add to frying pan. Mash beans coarsely with a potato masher or back of a fork. Add **1 t. salt,** and continue to cook, stir, and mash beans. Add as much **oil** as you like. Ample oil makes refried beans taste rich. Add reserved bean liquid as beans start to dry out and thicken. Do not mash mixture too smooth. Cover pan and cook over low heat for an additional 15 minutes to develop the flavor. Taste for **salt,** and serve topped with chopped **red onion.**

Serves 6-8

SPANISH RICE

1) Bring to a boil **2 c. white rice** and **3 c. water** in a covered pot. As soon as the water boils, turn the heat down and cook rice slowly until water is absorbed. Do not overcook.

2) Meanwhile, finely chop **1 medium onion** and mince **2 cloves garlic.** In a large frying pan saute onion, garlic, and ½ **t. cumin** in **3 Tb. olive oil** until slightly browned. Add ⅔ **c.** chopped **canned tomatoes,** and continue cooking until most of the liquid has evaporated.

3) Next, turn the cooked rice into the frying pan. Add **2 Tb. shoyu** and fry, stirring continuously, until all seasonings are thoroughly blended with rice. Cover and set aside until ready to serve.

Serves 6-8

. . . teen-age drifter can walk in hell
Or roll on the back room floor.
And the battered children who bruise and bleed
The mothers with too many kids to feed
Pro-Life offers them in their need
Back alley abortions for the poor.

"Back Alley Surgery"
Mama Lion
©*1978 Malvina Reynolds, Schroder Music*

POLENTA WITH
CAPER MISO SAUCE

1) Make **Polenta** (see recipe index) and turn out onto
   2 large dinner plates to make 2 thin rounds. Cool,
   cover with plastic wrap, and refrigerate.

2) Make **Caper Miso Sauce** (see recipe index) and
   keep warm in a covered pot.

3) Wipe clean and slice **3 c. mushrooms.** Fry in
   2 Tb. oil over highest heat, stirring constantly,
   until mushrooms stop giving up their liquid and
   have browned well. Add **salt** and **pepper** to taste.
   Set aside.

4) Slice each round of polenta in 6-7 wedges. Dredge
   each wedge in **flour** and fry in **1-2 Tb. oil** in a very
   hot frying pan until polenta has browned on both
   sides. Don't fry more pieces than will fit comfortably in
   frying pan. Remove polenta to a shallow pan. Repeat
   until all wedges are browned and crisp.

5) Thinly slice ½ **lb. mozzarella cheese.** Arrange
   on polenta. Top with mushrooms. Preheat broiler.
   Finely chop ¼ **c. straight leaf parsley** and **2 Tb.
   garlic leaves,** if available. Briefly broil polenta until
   cheese melts.

6) To serve, arrange 2 wedges polenta on each plate.
   Top with sauce, chopped parsley, and garlic leaves.
   Serve with a **tossed salad.**

Serves 6-7

BRANDIED BREAD PUDDING

A good use for stale homemade bread.

1) You will need enough **stale bread** to measure **5 c.** once it is cut into cubes. Rye and wholewheat are not as good for this recipe as oatmeal or white bread. Put the cubes in a buttered pan large enough to hold the pudding (it should hold at least 12 c. of liquid). Cover with **5½ c. milk** and let rest 2 hours or more.

2) Rinse **1 c. raisins,** gently squeeze moisture out, and barely cover them with **brandy** in a small bowl. Set aside.

3) Melt **4 Tb. sweet butter** in a small pot. In a bowl whisk together **5 eggs, ⅓ c. sugar, 1½ t. vanilla extract,** and ¾ **t. salt.** Stir cooled butter into egg mixture.

4) Mix raisins and brandy into eggs and pour over bread and milk. Stir well. Grate some **fresh nutmeg** over pudding. Bake at 325° about 1 hour or until custard is set.

5) Make **Brandy Sauce** to serve with Bread Pudding: Melt **8 Tb. butter** in a small pot. Set aside. In another pot whisk **2 eggs, ½ c. sugar,** and ½ **c. brandy.** Cook over moderate to low heat, whisking constantly, until mixture thickens a little the way a hollandaise sauce would. This will take about 10 minutes. Add melted butter gradually, still whisking. Remove from heat and cool. If the brandied sauce seems too thick, thin with a little **cream.** Refrigerate.

6) Bread pudding is best served warm. Individual servings can be reheated in a toaster oven. Serve in a saucer with brandied sauce around it.

Serves 9-10

How did they get there? (Man create the darkness)
How did they get there? (that they just don't see) . . .

Woman sees the signs,
Cradle in the darkness.
Woman sees the signs,
Chase away the darkness . . .

Oh, Mothers, Sisters, Daughters
Oh, Mothers, Sisters, Daughters

"Woman Who Sees The Signs"
Running
© 1983 June Millington; Fabulous Records

LEMON HONEY GALATOBOUREKO

A variation on a classic Greek pastry.

1) Warm **6 eggs** by placing them in a bowl, still in their shells, and covering them with hot tap water.

2) In a middle-sized pot, gently heat **2½ c. milk** with ½ **c. honey.** In a separate pitcher, stir together ½ **c. milk** and ¼ **c. cornstarch.** Set aside.

3) Break warmed eggs into mixer. Grate **rind** from **1½ lemons** and add to mixer. Beat eggs on highest speed while squeezing **juice** from **5-6 lemons.** Strain juice and measure it: you will need ¾ **c.** Set aside.

4) When milk comes to a simmer, stir cornstarch mix again and add, whisking after it comes to a boil for 1 full minute. Add lemon juice to mixer; turn mixer speed down and gradually add hot milk while the machine is running. Return custard to pot and simmer, stirring well, until it is quite thick. Remove from heat and stir another full minute. Cool 10 minutes. Chill in refrigerator ½ hour.

5) Make syrup: Bring **2 c. water** and ¾ **c. honey** to a boil. Add the **thin yellow peel** of **1 lemon** and simmer 15 minutes. Remove from heat and let cool. Set aside. Preheat oven to 375°.

6) Melt ¼ **lb. sweet butter** in a small pot. Use a brush
   to butter a 9″ x 12″ x 2″ shallow baking pan. Open a
   1 lb. package filo pastry and divide it in half. You
   can cut it with a knife if the filo will then fit best into
   your pan, or you can plan to fold the sheets, first to
   one side and then to the other. Brush each sheet,
   folded or not, with butter as you lay it into the pan. Try
   to be as neat as you can. When half the filo is in, turn
   the cooled custard over it. Now add the remaining
   sheets of filo, buttering each one. If you have had prior
   experience with filo, you will know that it becomes
   dried out quickly and should be kept between sheets
   of waxed paper under a dampened towel if there are to
   be delays of more than a few seconds.

7) When Galatoboureko has been completely
   assembled, cut part way into the pastry to make
   diamond shapes. A kitchen scissors will do the cross
   cuts better than a knife. Bake at 375° for about 1
   hour or until browned. Remove from oven and use
   knife to complete the diamond cuts. Pour syrup
   over the Galatoboureko, using only as much as you
   like to sweeten and moisten the pastry, but not so
   much that it becomes soggy.

Serves 12-15

BLACK BOTTOM
PINEAPPLE TOFU PIE

A rich and delicious dairy free "cheese" cake. It takes time and effort to make, but is worth the effort.

1) To make crust: Oil a baking pan measuring about 10" x 12". Preheat oven to 350°. Use a food processor to coarsely chop **1 c. almonds.** Turn into a small bowl. Put into processor: ½ **c. oil,** ½ **c. honey, 1 t. vanilla,** and ½ **c. roasted carob powder.** Turn machine on and off until blended. Add ⅔ **c. whole wheat flour** and ½ **t. baking powder** to machine, together with the chopped almonds and **2½ Tb. water.** Mix minimally. Use a metal spatula to scrape into the prepared pan and spread thinly. Bake in preheated oven until edges pull away from pan and top is no longer soft and sticky, about 15 minutes. Remove from oven.

2) Meanwhile measure **1½ c. pineapple coconut juice** (we use juices from health food sources) into a pot and sprinkle **2 Tb. agar-agar flakes** over juice. Turn fire to moderate, so that agar-agar flakes will soften before juice comes to a boil. Simmer uncovered for about 5 minutes.

3) Measure out ¾ **c. dried coconut,** ½ **c. walnuts,**
   and ¼ **c. filberts.** Nuts must be finely ground. Use a
   coffee mill, if you have one. Good texture in this
   dessert will come from well pulverized nuts. When
   finely ground, add to washed processor. Grate **rind** of
   1½ lemons over nuts. Turn machine on and add **1 c.
   oil,** a few drops at a time. Alternate with pieces of
   ½ **lb. tofu** and **juice** of **1½ lemons.** This must be
   done very gradually. Also add ½ **t. salt, 1 Tb.
   vanilla extract,** and ¼ **c. honey** or **maple
   syrup.** Mixture should turn white and be very thick.

4) When agar-agar and juice are ready (agar-agar seems
   to have dissolved), add to mixture in processor. Blend
   all together well. Pour over black bottom crust. Set
   aside while preparing pineapple topping.

5) You will need ½ of a **large ripe pineapple.** Cut into
   small, thin slices and put into the same unwashed pot
   used to heat juice. Add ¾ **c.** more **pineapple
   coconut juice** and bring to a boil. Separately mix
   1¼ Tb. arrowroot or cornstarch with ⅓ **c.** more
   juice until blended. Stir into hot pineapple mixture
   until clear and thickened. Spoon this topping over pie.
   Chill until ready to serve.

Yields about 12 servings

APRICOT CUSTARD CAKE

A sugar free sponge cake. The filling may be used in a pie shell and topped with whipped cream.

1) Make **Apricot Filling:** Use French chef's knife or shears to dice **½ lb. dried apricots.** Put into a pot with **2⅓ c. milk** and bring gently to a boil (milk will curdle). In a bowl mix **3⅓ Tb. cornstarch, ⅛ t. salt,** and **⅓ c. milk.** Add to milk-apricot mixture, stirring until thickened and smooth. Remove from heat.

2) In a bowl whisk **3 egg yolks, 1 whole egg,** and **3 Tb. maple syrup.** Gradually add hot mixture, stirring well. Return to pot and heat gently, stirring, until eggs have further thickened the custard. Turn off heat and flavor with **scant ½ t. almond extract, ¾ t. vanilla extract,** and **3 Tb. Jamaican rum.** Chill.

3) Make cake: Preheat oven to 325°. Warm **6 eggs** (in their shells) in a bowl of **hot water.** Butter three 9″ cake pans and line each with waxed paper. Scrape rind and squeeze juice of **2 oranges.** You should have **½ c. juice.**

4) If you have a food processor, separate eggs so that whites go into mixer and yolks into processor. Or simply put yolks into a bowl. Measure out ⅓ **c. unbleached white flour.** Whisk yolks (or run machine), adding ¼ **t. salt,** until thick and light. Add ½ **c. honey,** orange juice plus rind, and mix well. Now add flour and whisk into yolks thoroughly. A processor makes this easy.

5) Add **1 t. cream of tartar** to whites and beat to soft peak stage. Add **2 Tb. honey** and beat to stiff peaks. Remove bowl from mixer and fold yolk-flour mixture gently but thoroughly into whites. Divide between the three pans. Bake until cakes shrink slightly from edges of pan. Remove and cool 5 minutes in pans on racks. Use small knife to loosen edges, then turn cakes out onto racks to cool completely.

6) Sprinkle cake layers with **apricot wine, plum wine,** or **golden sherry.** Fill with apricot filling and chill. This cake is best served the next day topped with **whipped cream:** Beat **2 c. heavy cream** with **1 Tb. maple syrup,** ½ **t. almond extract,** and **1 Tb. apricot wine** or **sherry.**

"Can you imagine a world without men?"
"No crime and lots of happy, fat women."

Mercy, its the revolution and I'm in my bathrobe
Nicole Hollander; St. Martin's Press

AMASAKE PINEAPPLE RICE PUDDING

You will need amasake, a Japanese fermented rice drink, for this unsweetened, dairy free dessert. It can be purchased at some health food stores or made at home (see following recipe).

1) put **1¾ c. short grain brown rice** in a pot with **1½ c. unsweetened canned pineapple juice** (you will need a total of 3 c. or 24 oz.), **2½ c. water,** and **1½ t. dried ginger.** Bring to a boil and simmer, covered, until rice is very soft, about 45 minutes, stirring often. Add **1 c. amasake** and bring to a boil again. Set aside.

2) In a separate pot bring ½ **lb. tofu** and **1 c. pineapple juice** to a boil. Lift tofu out and place in food processor. Add ¾ **salt** and grated **rind** of **1 lemon.** Process until tofu is smoothly pureed, then add **2 Tb. oil,** ½ t. **vanilla extract, 1 t. cinnamon, 2 t. lemon juice,** and **1 c. amasake.** Scrape down sides of processor and turn on again to mix contents.

3) Add **1½ Tb. agar-agar flakes** and **1 c. water** to juice remaining in pot used to cook tofu. Stir well and bring to a boil. Simmer 3 minutes, then turn off heat and add ½ **c. raisins.** Let sit 5 minutes.

4) Cut ⅓ or a **large, ripe pineapple** into small dice
   (using remainder for other uses). In a bowl or large
   container, combine cooked rice, tofu mixture, raisin
   and agar-agar mix, diced pineapple and remaining
   juice. Mix well. Taste for **lemon juice** and **salt.**
   Chill.

Serves 10

*Everything in life is part of it . . . while on the surface
this may seem self-evident, the favorite conceit of male
culture is that experience can be fractured literally its
bones split . . . intellect from feeling and/or imagination;
act from consequence; symbol from reality; mind from
body . . . so the scientist can work on bomb or virus,
the artist on poem with no appreciation of its meaning
outside itself; . . . Even when faced with the probable
extinction of themselves at their own hand, men refuse
to look at the whole . . .*

Pornography Men Possessing Women
Andrea Dworkin; Putnam

AMASAKE

A form of fermented rice used instead of a sweetener and as a leavening agent in macrobiotic cooking. This recipe is from Ann Alves. We have not made amasake ourselves, since we buy it from our local tofu dairy. Koji, a mold called *Aspergillus oryzae,* is the starter needed to make amasake. It can be obtained from Mountain Ark Trading Co., 120 South Cast Street, Fayetteville, Arkansas 72701; Erewhon, 236 Washington Street, Brookline, Massachusetts 02146; or Chico-San, Inc., P.O. Box 810, Chico, California 95927. Refrigerate to keep.

1) Wash **4 c. sweet brown rice** well. Soak overnight in **8 c. water.**

2) Pressure cook rice in its soaking water for 20 minutes. Turn off heat and let sit unopened for 45 minutes. Turn rice into a glass or ceramic bowl (not metal). When it is cool enough to handle, add ½ **c. koji.** Mix well, using your hands.

3) Cover bowl with dish towel and let mixture ferment for about 4 hours. Stir several times, using hands or wooden spoon (not metal). Fermentation liquid will rise to the top. When it tastes very sweet, amasake is ready.

4) Turn into a pot, add a **pinch** of **salt** and bring to a boil. This stops fermentation. Cool and refrigerate in glass containers.

5) This amount of amasake should yield 2 qt., so if necessary add **water** when amasake is cool, and put through food processor or blender. If turned into a heavy pot, placed over a very low flame, and cooked to a rich tan color, amasake will become sweeter and will have a longer refrigerator shelf life.

6) Amasake may be flavored with **ginger juice, cinnamon,** or **dried tangerine peel** and served as a beverage. For most Westerners, this is an acquired taste. We like it as a sweetening and leavener in breads or as a base for rice puddings.

And just as male obstetricians took control of childbirth, and male doctors and funeral directors took control of dying and death (also once women's province), male professionals and manufacturers are eager to control our relationship to aging.
It's time to refuse to let men define either the social world of old women or our life process. We need to build a vision of our own — one that goes beyond either commercial exploitation or the patchwork "solutions" of family. We need to reclaim the value and meaning of our entire lifespans up to and including death.

"Aging, Ageism and Feminist Avoidance"
Cynthia Rich
Look Me In The Eye
Old Women, Aging, and Ageism
Barbara Macdonald with Cynthia Rich
Spinsters Ink

ANN ALVES' SWEET
RICE PUDDING

1) Pressure cook **5 c. sweet brown rice** in **7 c. apple juice, water, Mu tea,** or a mixture of the three. Also add **pinch salt, 1 cinnamon stick,** and a split **vanilla bean.** Cook 45 minutes.

2) Meanwhile toast **2 c. almonds** in a 375° oven 10-15 minutes. Cool, slice.

3) Simmer **3 c. dried fruits** (such as apricots, raisins, prunes, and apples) in a small amount of **water** with a **pinch** of **salt** until softened.

4) Combine in a shallow casserole: the cooked rice, **4 c. amasake,** fruit, and nuts. Bake in a 350° oven, covered, for 30 minutes. Uncover and top with **grated lemon rind.** Bake until top browns.

Serves 10-12

Skin. Wet. Women are so wet: tears, sweat, juice. We must have come from the sea. Soft. Very sweet.

"Ebbs And Flows"
The Reach and other stories: lesbian feminist fiction
Gillian E. Hanscombe; Ed:Lilian Mohin and Sheila Shulman

ORANGE APRICOT
TOFU MOUSSE

1) Make the same tofu mousse base as described in the recipe for **Cranberry Tofu Mousse** (see recipe index).

2) Cut up and soak **1 c. dried apricots** in **1 c. water** for 2 hours. If still hard, bring gently to a boil. Cool. Peel and slice **2 oranges** and add to apricots. Taste this sauce and add **maple syrup** if it seems to need sweetening. Since the mousse itself is sweet, the fruit sauce which tops it should be somewhat tart. Finally, peel and slice **2 kiwi fruit,** if you like, to mix into the sauce. Chill and serve over mousse.

Serves 6

You say I am mysterious.
Let me explain myself:
In a land of oranges
I am faithful to apples.

"You Say"
Sapphic Songs
Elsa Gidlow; Druid Heights Books

~~~~~~~~~~~~~~~~~~~~~~~~

CHAPTER 3   SPRING

And we are enveloped in a powerful, sweet odor that transforms the night . . . Sniffing the air, we seek the source — and find it. The cornfield in bloom. Row on row of sturdy stalks, with their tassels held up to the moon. Silently, in slow rhythm, we make our way into the field. The faint rustle of growing plants flows around and through us, until, when we stop by a tall stalk, there seems no division between flesh and green. We rub the smooth, sinewy leaves on our cheeks and touch a nubile ear, where each grain of pollen that falls from the tassel will make a kernel, strong and turgid with milk. Linking arms around the stalk, we lift our faces to the drifting pollen and breathe the spirit of the Corn Woman — the powerful, joyous, nurturing odor of one complete-in-herself.

"Where are your women?"
We are here.

Marilou Awiakta
"Amazons in Appalachia"
Sinister Wisdom 22/23 A Gathering of Spirit

MULLIGATAWNY SOUP

Made from red lentils and coconut milk.

1) Wash **2 c. red lentils** and cover with **water** to soak
   for about 30 minutes. Red lentils are available in health
   food stores, Middle Eastern markets or Indian
   markets, where they are known as masur dahl.

2) Drain lentils and turn into a soup pot. Add **2 qt.
   water** and bring to a boil. Skim foam from surface.
   Tie a **few whole cloves, 2 bay leaves,** and a
   few whole peppercorns in cheesecloth, and add
   to pot along with **1 Tb. tumeric, 4** peeled **cloves
   garlic, 1 t. whole cumin seed,** and **1 small
   fresh hot chili pepper.** Simmer, covered, 1 to 1½
   hours.

3) While lentils cook, measure ¾ **c. dried coconut**
   into blender or food processor. Add **1 c.** of hottest
   possible **tap water,** and pulverize thoroughly. Turn
   into a strainer over a bowl and squeeze handfuls of
   coconut to extract the milk. Discard pulp. Reserve
   milk.

4) When lentils are cooked, remove cheesecloth and
   puree soup in several batches in blender or processor.
   Return to soup pot. Add **1 Tb. salt, 2 Tb. lime** or
   lemon juice, and coconut milk. Correct seasoning.
   If soup seems too thick, dilute with **water.** Garnish
   with a **slice** of **lime** or **lemon** in each bowl.

Serves 6-8

SESAME CELERY SOUP

From Lucy Lloyd of La Papaya, a feminist vegetarian
restaurant which used to be in Brooklyn, New York.

1) Coarsely chop stalks and upper leaves to measure
   4 c. celery. Slice **2 c. onions.** Turn both into soup
   pot with **2 Tb. oil** and **1 Tb. Chinese sesame oil.**
   Fry over high heat until vegetables begin to brown
   slightly.

2) Add ⅓ **t. dried ginger** and **3 Tb. flour.** Cook,
   stirring well, for a few minutes.

3) Add **2 qt. water, 3 Tb. dry sherry,** ¼ **c. tahini,**
   (sesame paste), ½ **c.** chopped **canned tomatoes,**
   ⅓ **c. shoyu,** and (optional) **1-2 t. Chinese chili
   paste with garlic** (available at Chinese markets).
   Bring to a boil and taste for seasoning. The soup may
   need a little **salt** and freshly ground **pepper.**

4) Serve garnished with fresh **cilantro,** available at
   Hispanic groceries or Chinese food stores.

Serves 8

NAVY BEAN &
SOUR CREAM SOUP

From Sharon Varga.

1) Soak **1½ lb. navy beans** in **water** to cover
   overnight, or lacking time, bring to a boil, turn off heat
   and leave covered for 1 hour. Flavor of soup is best
   when beans are soaked overnight.

2) Drain beans, cover with **2 qt. water.** Add **5 bay
   leaves** and simmer until beans are tender.

3) Give soup a sour flavor by adding **white vinegar** to
   taste, about **3 Tb.** Whisk **1 Tb. flour** into **2 c.
   sour cream** and add to soup. Cook 15 minutes more.
   Season with **2 t. salt** and freshly ground **pepper.**
   Taste to correct seasonings and sourness.

4) If you like, this soup can be pureed in a blender. Chill
   and serve cold with a garnish of chopped **raw onions.
   Rye bread** is a good accompaniment to this soup.

                                              Serves 8

SCANDINAVIAN FRUIT SOUP

We are all hungry for fresh fruit when winter is over but it is still too early for spring fruits. Here is a dried fruit soup for a warm day in Spring. Save some for **Fruit Compote French Toast** (see recipe index).

1) Dice **1½ c. dried apricots, 1 c. dried prunes,** and trim cores and dice **2 c. dried apples.** Turn into a stainless steel pot, and cover with **10 c. water.** Let stand 30 minutes.

2) Add **2 whole sticks cinnamon, ½ lemon** (both juice and rind, but not pits), **1 t. ground cardamom,** and ⅓ **c. quick cooking tapioca.** Bring to a boil and simmer, stirring occasionally, for about 10 minutes. Turn off heat.

3) Add ¼ **c. raisins** and ¼ **c. currants** to hot soup. Season with **1 scant t. salt.** Cool, chill.

4) If soup is too thick at serving time, dilute with **water** or **apple juice.** Serve with **sour cream** if you like.

Serves 7-8

HIZIKI OR ARAME SALAD NEST

Arame means "tough maiden", comparing this seaweed to the Japanese women who dive for pearls. You may find it less available than the more expensive Hiziki.

1) To sort for little stones or shells, turn about **1 qt. Arame** or **Hiziki** into a large bowl. Cover with **cold water.** Swish sea vegetable through the water and lift out into a colander. Check bottom of bowl for stones or shells and discard. Repeat 3 times, using fresh water each time. Washing also removes much of the fishy flavor. Turn drained sea vegetable into a soup pot, add **3 c. water** to barely cover, **2 Tb. honey, 3 Tb. shoyu,** and bring to boil. Simmer about 1 hour. Taste for flavor and add more **honey** or **shoyu** as needed. When sea vegetable is well fluffed, turn it and the cooking liquid into a container. Cool, cover, and chill.

2) Combine ½ **c. water,** ¼ **c. rice wine vinegar, 2 Tb. shoyu,** and **1 Tb. honey** in a small pot. Bring to a boil. Cool, chill.

3) When marinade has cooled, peel, seed and dice **1 cucumber.** Add to marinade and refrigerate.

4) When ready to serve, use a slotted spoon to lift sea
   vegetable onto each plate. Shape into a nest. Drain
   some cucumber and add to nest. Dice ½ **lb. tofu**
   (preferably soft tofu), and add some cubes to each
   nest. Surround sea vegetable with **watercress
   leaves.** You will need about **2 bunches** in all. Spoon
   marinade over cress, as well as a **few drops** of
   Chinese sesame oil. Sprinkle tofu with **Gomahsio**
   (see recipe index).

Serves 6

And speaking of The Boys, *aren't we ever going to try
to put it together as to just why he likes being with
them better than he likes being with you? But even
more importantly, aren't we ever going to get together
as to just why he's so afraid of our getting together with
The Girls? And especially with the white girls? Which
brings me right square to where I want to be which is
with our white, brown, and black Sisters in Womyn's
Liberation which The Boys call Womyn's Lib and which
they also hate like homemade sin because they know
Womyn's Liberation is going to set our heads free.*

Black Lesbian in White America
Anita Cornwall; Naiad

PASTA PRIMAVERA SALAD

For a taste of early Spring, you may hunt wild herbs to flavor this salad or use some domesticated ones from your garden. Some cooks will have to depend on the sadder resource of the supermarket.

1) Fresh cavatelli has the best texture and the look of Spring fertility, though dried pasta shells, or other shapes may be substituted. Cavatelli is usually available in Italian neighborhoods. Put up a large pot of **water** to boil with **1 Tb. salt.** When boiling, add **1 lb. fresh cavatelli** or ¾ lb. dried pasta. Cook until barely done, tasting pasta to be sure it is still "al dente". Drain in a colander, and run cold water over until cooled. Shake colander vigorously, and turn pasta into a bowl. Add **2 Tb.** good quality **imported olive oil** and **2 scant Tb. shoyu.** Toss together well.

2) Gather herbs. You will need ⅔ **c. sorrel,** finely chopped, to give the salad a tart taste, **1 Tb. watercress,** minced, for a mustard flavor, **1 Tb. garlic leaves,** and **1 ½ Tb. onion tops,** chopped. Turn the herbs into bowl with pasta and toss well.

3) Toast ⅓ **c. walnuts** in a toaster oven until they smell good and begin to change color. Let cool and then chop coarsely. Drain **1 small can pitted olives** and coarsely chop enough to measure ⅓ c. Add nuts and olives to pasta. Mince ½ **small tabasco pepper** very fine, and stir into ¼ **c. Vinaigrette** (see recipe index). Add to pasta and toss well.

4) This salad is best served at room temperature, but may be chilled. Serve on **lettuce** with a drizzle of vinaigrette, garnished with a slice of **red onion**.

Serves 4 heartily

the first person I loved
was a woman   my passion
for her lasted thirty years
and was not returned
she never let me suck her nipples
she kept secrets between her legs
she told me men would love me
for myself   she couldn't tell me
ways to love myself
she didn't know

Mother, I would like to help you
swim back against the foaming river
to the source of our
incestuous fears
but you're so tired
out beyond the breakers
and I am upstream among my sisters
spawning.

"Coming Out"
Jacqueline Lapidus
Lesbian Poetry
Ed: Elly Bulkin and Joan Larkin; Persephone Press

WILD RICE SALAD

Since we do without meat, vegetarians can sometimes splurge on this precious and delicious fruit of the wild aquatic grass, *Zizania aquatica*. It is gathered by the Ojibwa (Chippewa) of the Great Lakes region who call themselves "Menominee" which means "wild rice people".

1) Wash **2½ c. wild rice** and drain in strainer or colander. Bring **4 c. water** and **1½ t. salt** to a boil. Add rice and cook, covered, over moderate heat for 35 minutes.

2) Scrape **carrots** and cut in thin ovals to measure **2½ c.** Prepare **2½ c. asparagus** by cutting into **¾"** pieces, and cut **2 c. celery** in the same manner. Set aside in separate bowls.

3) In a stainless steel pot combine following marinade: **½ c. water, ½ c. wine vinegar, ½ c. apple juice, 1½ t. salt, ½ t. dried thyme, 2 bay leaves, 1 clove** crushed **garlic,** and **½ c. olive oil.**

4) Bring marinade to a boil and add carrots. Simmer 3 minutes. Add asparagus and celery, and simmer 2 more minutes. Add **1 t. prepared mustard** to pot and stir well.

5) Immediately pour vegetables into a colander over a bowl so that they do not continue cooking.

6) Add marinade to wild rice when it is done cooking. Cool rice and vegetables separately. When cooled, combine, adding **1 Tb. lemon juice** and **1 t. salt.** Chill.

7) To serve, arrange rice on leaves of **Boston lettuce.** Top with slivered, toasted **almonds,** and garnish with **watercress.**

Serves 8

The gradual overlay of culture on nature in prehistoric times; the subsequent overlay of physical nature on that "pagan" culture when the earth reclaimed its ruins and, with them, ancient (often matriarchal) beliefs; and now the overlay of our new perceptions of the culture lying beneath the "almost natural" forms — all this suggests a powerful merger of the two elements from which art springs. It is all the more tantalizing to feminists, working to understand where nature got separated from culture and how women became associated with an "inferior" natural line.

Overlay
Lucy R. Lippard; Pantheon Books

FEIJOADA

This elaborate Brazilian meal of rice and beans has
African origins. Traditionally served with a variety of
meats, we find the other customary accompaniments
adequate in producing a satisfying dinner.

1) Cover **2 c. black turtle beans** with **water** and
   soak overnight. Or lacking time, bring to a boil,
   remove from heat and let stand, covered, for 1 hour.
   Prepare **Fried Kale** and **Manioc** (see following
   recipes). Hard boil **3 eggs.**

2) Drain beans, cover with fresh **water,** and simmer
   until tender.

3) Chop **2 medium onions,** and thinly slice **4 red
   peppers.** Turn into sauce pot and saute with
   3 Tb. oil. Add **2 t. oregano, 4 t. cumin,** and **4
   cloves** crushed **garlic.**

4) When vegetables are soft and golden, add the cooked
   turtle beans, **2 Tb. lemon juice,** ¼ **c. red wine,**
   and **1 c. canned tomatoes.** Add **salt** and **pepper**
   to taste. Cover and simmer 30 minutes.

5) In a separate pan cook **1½ c. long grain white
   rice** in **2½ c. water** with **1 t. salt.** Set aside.

6) Prepare **Lemon Pepper Hot Sauce:** Finely chop
enough **onion** to measure ¼ **c.** Continue using a
good French chef's knife to chop **1 clove garlic** and
2 bottled tabasco peppers, mincing all very fine.
Turn into a bowl and add ¼ **c.** freshly squeezed
lemon juice.

7) Finish beans by stirring in **3 Tb. dark rum.** Serve
beans over rice with kale and manioc on the side.
Brazilians reputedly sprinkle manioc over Feijoada.
Use the Lemon Pepper Sauce if you like spicy food.
Garnish plates or platter with **hard boiled eggs,** cut
in half, and **black olives.**

Serves 6

*Perhaps the Amazons who rode into Europe from the
Russian steppes were fierce, blonde blue-eyed women.
My Amazons have always been dark . . .
The dark-skinned women who rode, thousands strong,
across the African continent and through the Arab
world are my reminder that I am the ancestral
daughter/sister of a powerful nation of women . . . For
me, this image has been an amazing source of courage,
conviction, and freedom.*

"The Goddess Heritage of Black Women"
Sabrina Sojourner
The Politics of Women's Spirituality
Ed: Charlene Spretnak; Doubleday

FRIED KALE FOR FEIJOADA

1) Bring **6 quarts** of **water** to a boil in a large pot.
   Meanwhile, remove stems from **3 lb. kale.** Shred
   kale into thin strips and then wash it thoroughly in
   cold running water.

2) When the water has boiled, add the shredded greens
   to the pot, and cook 3 minutes. Drain in colander,
   pressing out as much excess liquid as possible.

3) In a large frying pan preheat **3 Tb. olive oil** over
   medium-high heat. Add the greens and fry, stirring
   constantly, for about 15 minutes. (The kale will turn
   from bright green to a dull dark green color.) Add
   1 large clove minced **garlic.** Fry 1 or 2 minutes
   more to cook the garlic, and then add **1 Tb. shoyu.**
   Continue frying until the shoyu liquid has evaporated.
   Taste for seasoning and add a little **salt** if necessary.

Serves 6 as a side dish

TOASTED MANIOC MEAL

A traditional topping for Feijoada is toasted manioc, a fine, grainlike meal made from a dried root, which is also known as cassava. It is available, packaged, in Latin American stores as Farinha de Mandioca. It is a nice addition, but not necessary to the dinner.

1) In a heavy frying pan over medium-low heat, dry roast **1 c. manioc meal,** stirring until pale brown. If available, add **1 Tb. dende** or **palm oil** (on sale in Latin American stores) or **butter,** and stir into the meal. Turn out into a heat proof bowl.

2) Finely chop **1 small onion.** Fork beat **1 egg** in a small bowl. Now melt **2 Tb. butter** in the same frying pan and saute the onions until transparent and beginning to turn golden. Add the egg and stir well. Return manioc to frying pan and mix all ingredients thoroughly. Turn off heat. Add **salt** to taste. Serve at room temperature.

TEMPEH STUFFED BAKED POTATOES

This is an easy and delicious way to serve tempeh.

1) Scrub **6 large Idaho potatoes** and bake in a 400° oven for about 1 hour or until tender.

2) Meanwhile, cut **1 cake tempeh** (8 oz.) into thin matchstick lengths, then crosswise into dice. Set aside. Chop **1½ medium onions, 1 large stalk celery** with **leaves**, and **2½ c. mushrooms.** In a large frying pan heat **2 Tb. cooking oil** and fry tempeh with vegetables over high heat, stirring often, until tempeh and mushrooms are crisped and brown. Meanwhile add ¾ **t. ground coriander, 1 clove** crushed **garlic,** ½ **Tb. salt,** and freshly ground **pepper.** When mixture is very well browned, turn off heat and stir in **3 Tb. dry sherry, 1½ Tb. lemon juice,** and ½ **c.** chopped **parsley.** Taste for seasoning. Set aside.

3) When potatoes are done, slice off ½" of the skin on top. Use a pointed spoon to scoop out about ¾ of each potato. Turn the potato pulp into a mixer to mash until fluffy. Add **2 Tb. sweet butter** and about ⅓-½ **c. milk** or enough to keep mixture soft and fluffy, but not too soft. Add **salt** and freshly ground **pepper** to taste. Briefly mix in cooled tempeh and vegetables. Don't overmix. Restuff potato shells. Sprinkle with **paprika** and refrigerate until serving time.

4) Though not essential, it is nice to serve these potatoes with **Miso Gravy** (see recipe index).

5) When ready to serve, heat potatoes for 20-30 minutes in a 400° oven or toaster oven. Meanwhile, cut **8 carrots** into matchsticks and steam until just done, about 10 minutes. Divide **1 head** of **broccoli** into flowerets and steam until done, about 5 minutes. In a small pot melt **4 Tb. sweet butter.** Peel **1 clove garlic** and lightly bruise it with the handle of a French chef's knife. Add to melted butter with **3 Tb. bread crumbs.** Cook over moderate heat until crumbs are somewhat browned. Remove and discard garlic clove.

6) When potatoes are heated through and tops look well browned and crisped, remove to serving plate. Add miso gravy if you like, and serve with steamed broccoli and carrots, garnished with the bread crumb butter.

Serves 6

There are Women everywhere with fragments
gather fragments
weave and mend
When we learn to come together we are whole
When we learn to recognize the enemy
we will know what we need to know
to learn how to come together
to learn how to weave and mend

Daughters of Copper Woman
Anne Cameron; Press Gang Publishers

SPINACH & MATZAH MEENA

A Sephardi Passover dish from Ethel Corey. Kashcaval cheese is Roumanian. It should be available at cheese stores.

1) Clean and shred **3 lb. spinach.** Dice **1 large onion.** Heat **3 Tb. olive oil** in a frying pan, and saute onion until golden. Add spinach in several batches, stirring each time, and cook until it wilts. Meanwhile add **2 Tb. fresh dill,** chopped. When all spinach is cooked, season mixture to taste with **salt,** freshly ground **pepper,** and **nutmeg.** Set aside.

2) Spread **8 whole matzahs** on trays in a single layer. Sprinkle with **water** to moisten, but don't let matzahs get so wet that they will fall apart when lifted.

3) Mix together ½ **lb. feta cheese,** crumbled, **3 c. cottage cheese, 1 lb. kashcaval,** grated, and **9** fork-beaten **eggs.** Add **2-3 t. salt,** to taste, considering the saltiness of the cheese. Add freshly ground **pepper.**

4) Pour **2 Tb. olive oil** in a 9" x 14" pan. Layer matzah in pan, cutting or breaking pieces to fit. Add half of the cheese mixture and another layer of matzah. Add half the spinach mixture, more matzah, remaining cheese, etc., ending with a layer of matzah.

5) Drizzle **2 Tb. olive oil** over the top of the spinach meena and bake in 375° oven for 30-40 minutes or until puffed and browned. Can be reheated or served cold as a snack.

Serves 12

Just as I was taught always to ask "Is it good for the Jews?" I now ask, "Is it good for women?" I do not understand the women who write about battered husbands and are then surprised that their data is used against battered women; who write about connections between rape and the menstrual cycle and are surprised when that too is used against women. I am never surprised. They are always looking for Christian babies' blood in the matzah. They will always use anything they can against us.

"How A Nice Jewish Girl Like Me Could"
Pauline Bart
Nice Jewish Girls; *Crossing Press*

POTATO KUGEL

Kugel means pudding. This is an easy to make, reheatable version of potato pancakes. Beating eggwhites stiff makes this kugel lighter and crisper than the traditional version of this recipe. Serve with Dried Apple Apricot Sauce and sour cream. A good Passover dish.

1) Prepare **Apple Apricot Sauce:** In a saucepan combine ½ **c. dried apricots, 1 c. dried apple slices,** and **2 c. apple juice.** Simmer, covered, until fruit is tender. Puree thoroughly in a food processor. Return to pot with **1½ c. water** and **4 fresh apples,** peeled, cored and thinly sliced. Simmer over low heat, covered, until apples are cooked. If sauce seems too stiff, thin with **water** or **apple juice.** Set aside.

2) Peel **3 large Idaho potatoes** and grate in processor or with hand grater. Do not use a blender. Also grate **1 medium-large onion.** Turn potato-onion mixture into a colander over a bowl and press gently to remove some liquid. Turn contents of colander into another bowl.

3) Preheat oven to 400° and place a metal baking pan that measures about 8″ by 15″ in oven. It is not wise to use Pyrex for this recipe. Add **2-3 Tb. oil** to pan.

4) To potato mixture add the following: **2 t. salt,** ½ **bunch** chopped **straight leaf parsley, 1½ Tb. potato starch,** freshly grated **pepper,** and **2 egg yolks.** Place the **egg whites** in a mixer.

5) Add **1-2 additional egg whites** to whites in mixer. Beat until stiff. Meanwhile, pour off the liquid squeezed from the potatoes into a cup. Add the potato starch accumulated at the bottom of the bowl to the potato-onion mixture and stir well with a wooden spoon. You may want to add some of the reserved liquid if mixture seems too stiff and dry. Consistency should be soft enough so that egg whites can be folded into mixture easily.

6) Add beaten whites to potatoes and use both clean hands, fingers spread apart, to "fold" whites into potatoes. This process is more like combing hair than like folding. Finally, wash your hands and turn kugel into the prepared hot baking dish. Bake 45 to 60 minutes or until kugel is puffed and crispy brown. Cut into wedges and serve with **Apple Apricot Sauce** and **sour cream.** Potato kugel reheats well or can be eaten cold for lunch or a snack.

Serves 4-5

I am sorry, Mother.
I named your anger. A woman's anger is not supposed to be named. A woman's anger is supposed to be cause for shame.

"A Book Of Travail — And Of A Humming
Under My Feet"
Barbara Deming
New Lesbian Writing
Ed: Margaret Cruikshank; Grey Fox Press

ARTICHOKES STUFFED WITH TOFU IN WHITE WINE & TARRAGON SAUCE

1) In a pot boil ¾ **c. water** with a **1½″ piece** of **kombu** (dried seaweed) for 10 minutes to make a broth.

2) Clean ¼ **lb. mushrooms.** Quarter and stew, covered, in ½ **c. water** for about 5 minutes.

3) In a stainless pot stew **1 lb. tofu,** cut into small pieces, in ⅓ **c. dry white wine,** ¼ **c. shoyu,** and **1 bay leaf** for about 5 minutes. Discard bay leaf.

4) Melt **3 Tb. butter.** Add ¼ **c. flour** and stir together until well blended. Add ¼ **c. milk** and all the drained liquid from the kombu, mushrooms, and tofu, setting aside the drained vegetables. Use whisk to stir this mixture until it comes to a simmer. Add ⅓ **t. dried tarragon,** crumbled, and a **pinch** of **thyme.** Add **salt** and **pepper** to taste, plus **1½ t. lemon juice.** Stir and taste for seasoning.

5) In a small bowl whisk together **2 egg yolks** and ¼ **c. heavy cream.** Slowly add hot sauce to yolks, stirring carefully so that yolks don't curdle. Finely dice kombu and stir into the finished sauce together with mushroom and tofu pieces. If sauce seems too stiff, thin with a little **cream.** Let cool.

6) Cut off stems and the top inch from **8 large artichokes.** Snip pointed tips from remaining leaves.

Cook artichokes in **boiling water** to cover until
they are just done (you can tell by pulling out a leaf
and tasting it to see if it's tender). Remove from water
with tongs and let cool until you can handle
artichokes.

7) Pull out some of the central leaves of each artichoke
and use a pointed teaspoon to scrape out and discard
the choke. Fill with tofu sauce. Serve immediately with
cooked **rice** and a **wedge** of **lemon.** Or refrigerate
until serving time and steam cold artichokes to reheat.
Remaining tofu sauce can be served over rice.

Serves 8

*"During the Golden Age, everyone in the terrestrial
garden was called amazon. Mothers were not distinct
from daughters. They lived in harmony and shared
pleasures . . .
"Then came a time when some daughters, and some
mothers did not like wandering anymore in the
terrestrial garden. They began to stay in the cities and
most often they watched their abdomens grow. This
activity brought them, it is said, great satisfaction.
Things went so far in this direction that they refused to
have any other interests. In vain, their friends asked
them to join them in their travels. They always had a
new abdomen to watch. Thus they called themselves
mothers."*

Lesbian Peoples: Material for a Dictionary
Monique Wittig and Sande Zeig; Avon

SWEET & SOUR TEMPEH

1) In a shallow container mix ⅔ **c. white wine,** ⅓ **c. tamari,** ⅓ **c. water, 2 cloves** crushed **garlic,** and ½ **t.** freshly grated **ginger.** Marinate **2 cakes of tempeh** (8 oz.) in this for several hours. Cut tempeh in half crosswise (each half will serve 1 person), and place in shallow frying pan with marinade. Stew, covered, for about 5 minutes. Cool. Place tempeh in covered container in refrigerator until time to serve, and reserve marinade separately.

2) Prepare **Sweet and Sour Sauce:** Combine in a bowl ¼ **c. vinegar, 2**½ **Tb. molasses,** ⅞ **c. water, 1 Tb. shoyu,** ⅔ **c. dry sherry, 2 Tb. cornstarch, 3 Tb. catsup** (we prefer Johnson's Table sauce), **1 Tb. Chinese sesame oil,** and **2 t.** freshly grated **ginger.** Dice pineapple from **1 small can unsweetened pineapple** and add with **juices.** Set aside.

3) Cut **2 carrots, 1**½ **green peppers,** and **3 scallions** into matchstick sized pieces. Peel and crush **3 cloves garlic.** Heat **1**½ **Tb. peanut oil** in frying pan. First fry carrots over highest heat, then add peppers and scallions, garlic last. Saute until browned but still crispy. Stir sauce mixture well and add, stirring. Bring to a boil and cook until thick and clear. Remove from heat and add reserved tempeh marinade. Cover to keep warm.

4) Prepare brown rice: Bring **2 c. short grain brown
   rice** and **3 c. water** to a boil in a pot with **scant t.
   salt.** Reduce heat to simmer and cook about 40
   minutes.

5) Preheat broiler. Place tempeh in oiled pan and brush
   tops with **oil.** Turn pieces until well browned/charcoal
   broiled. Slice each cake into matchstick pieces and
   place over rice. Top with Sweet and Sour Sauce and
   sliced **scallions.** If available, serve with **Kim Chi**
   (see following recipe).

Serves 4

*As Jewish women, we need to look at our people with
our own eyes. To see Judith, who saved the Jewish
people; she flirted with the attacking general, drank
him under the table; then she and her maid (whose
name is not in the story) whacked off his head, stuck it
in a picnic basket and escaped back to the Jewish
camp. They staked his head high over the gate, so that
when his soldiers charged the camp, they were met by
their general's bloody head, looming; and ran away as
fast as their goyishe little feet could run. Then Judith set
her maid free, and all the women danced in her honor.
That's a Jewish princess.*

"Some Notes on Jewish Lesbian Identity"
Melanie Kaye/Kantrowitz
Nice Jewish Girls
Ed: Evelyn Torton Beck; Crossing Press

KIM CHI

This spicy Korean version of sauerkraut is a condiment we like to serve with **Sweet and Sour Tempeh**. It needs about 5 days to ferment.

1) Cut **1 large Chinese cabbage** in quarters, then eighths, and finally into 1″ pieces. Put into large bowl and sprinkle with **2 Tb. sea salt**. Let stand 15 minutes.

2) In a very large (5 qt.) jar or crock put the following ingredients: Cut **1 bunch scallions** in half lengthwise and then crosswise into 1″ pieces. Add **1 large clove** crushed **garlic, 1 large cucumber,** peeled and sliced, **1 Tb. tumeric, 1½ Tb. hot pepper flakes,** and **1 t.** freshly grated **ginger root.**

3) Thoroughly rinse cabbage in cold running water by covering with fresh water and draining 3 times. Put drained cabbage into jar or crock, pushing down on contents. Add **water** to barely cover, then add **1 Tb. sea salt**. Stir as well as you can.

4) Cover and let ferment 3-5 days at room temperature, stirring at least once a day. When cabbage develops a typical sauerkraut flavor, refrigerate.

GREEN GODDESS SOUFFLE

An elegant introduction to Spring.

1) To prepare liquid and vegetables for souffle base, first
   snap off the tough lower stalks from **1 lb. asparagus**
   and barely cover with **water;** cook until stalks are soft.
   Drain, pressing down on stalks to get good flavor into
   the liquid. Discard the stalks. Dice the upper tender
   parts of the asparagus and cook very briefly in the
   reserved asparagus liquid until just done. Again drain
   liquid and set aside. You should have 2 c. asparagus
   pieces. Wash ½ **lb. fresh spinach** and steam in the
   liquid that clings to the leaves. Puree in food processor
   or blender and strain well. Add spinach to asparagus
   pieces, drained liquid to asparagus liquid, and set both
   aside. You will need 1 c. liquid in all.

2) Dice **2 Tb. shallots** and **1 clove garlic** (or more
   preferably, **1 Tb. garlic leaves**). Saute in **3 Tb.
   unsalted butter.** Add ¼ **t. dry mustard, 1 t.
   ground coriander,** and ¼ **t. ground cumin.** When
   shallots have softened and are light brown, add
   ⅓ **c. flour.** Cook together, stirring, until well
   blended. Add 1 c. of the reserved liquid and ⅓ **c. dry
   white wine.** Whisk mixture well over low heat. It will
   get quite thick. Remove from heat and let cool 10
   minutes, stirring occasionally.

3) Meanwhile, separate **6 eggs.** Be very careful not to get any yolks into the whites, or souffle will not rise well. Set whites aside. Stir the yolks into the shallot butter and flour mixture. Mix well. Add ⅓ **c. grated Parmesan cheese,** a **little** freshly grated **nutmeg, 1 Tb. shoyu,** ¾ **Tb. lemon juice,** and freshly ground **pepper.** Finally, fold in reserved cooked vegetables, using a slotted spoon to be sure not to add residual liquid. Taste for seasoning. Refrigerate this souffle base until dinner time. Also refrigerate the reserved egg whites. Prepare **Herbed Sour Cream Sauce** (see following recipe).

4) Let egg whites come to room temperature (about ½ hour) before beating. You will need another **6 egg whites** to make a light, puffy souffle. Preheat oven to 400° and butter 1 large souffle dish, 1 straight sided casserole, or 3-4 individual dishes. Any ovenproof casserole will do. You will need 1 c. of souffle base and ½ c. unbeaten egg white to serve each diner. Beat egg whites in a mixer until soft peaks form. Do not beat until stiff, dry peaks form. Fold souffle base and whites together—you should not be thorough—and turn into prepared pans. Sprinkle tops with grated **Parmesan cheese** and put into preheated oven. Lower heat to 375° and bake until souffle is puffed and brown, about 25-35 minutes. Since it will fall after that, serve immediately, with the sauce.

Serves 3-4

HERBED SOUR CREAM SAUCE

Stir together **1 c. sour cream,** ½ **Tb. horseradish,** ½ **Tb. lemon juice,** and **1 Tb. shoyu.** Fresh herbs are what makes this sauce exceptional. Cloves of garlic planted the Autumn before will yield mild flavored garlic leaves in spring. Chop enough **garlic leaves** to measure **2 Tb.** and add to sauce with **1 Tb.** chopped **straight leaf parsley, 1 Tb.** chopped **watercress leaves,** and ½ **Tb.** chopped **dill.** Taste for seasoning. If you have no garlic leaves, do not substitute cloves of garlic. Refrigerate.

Somewhere in the mind of the human race is the memory of who we are and what we represent. The cultures that produced thousands of images of fat women knew this about us, that we represent the ultimate female, full, round, big, strong, soft, warm woman. The moon is round, the earth is round, cycles are round, and so are we.

"The Goddess is Fat"
Kelly
Shadow on a Tightrope
Ed: Lisa Schoenfielder and Barb Wieser;
Aunt Lute Book Company

PASTA WITH
ARTICHOKE ASPARAGUS SAUCE
& GREMOLATA

A good way to use up small amounts of spring vegetables.
Already cooked ones are fine, if you have been careful to
save the cooking water.

1) Trim **2 artichokes.** Barely cover with **water** and cook
   until tender. Remove from broth to cool. Snap off hard
   bottoms of ½ **lb. asparagus.** Be sure bottoms are clean
   before adding them to artichoke broth. Simmer to
   extract flavor. Since you will need 5-6 c. broth, judge
   whether you should cover the pot or leave it
   uncovered to reduce the liquid.

2) Slice asparagus stalks thinly and set aside. Scrape
   flesh from each artichoke leaf, trim off choke and slice
   base. Set aside in a separate bowl.

3) In a sauce pot stew **2 cloves** minced **garlic** in ⅓ c.
   olive oil. Add ⅓ **c. flour** and stir while cooking for
   a minute or two. Gradually add strained broth, using
   as much as seems appropriate, whisking the mixture
   together as it simmers. Season with **1-2 Tb. shoyu,**
   2-3 t. lemon juice, some freshly ground **pepper,**
   and little **nutmeg.** Taste for seasoning. Sauce
   should be thin. Now add reserved asparagus, cover
   and simmer 5-10 minutes until tender. Add reserved
   artichoke flesh, stir together, and set sauce aside.

4) Toast ½ c. **pignoli nuts** in the oven until golden brown.
   Crush with a rolling pin.

5) Make **Gremolata:** Chop together finely ½ **c. straight leaf parsley,** ⅓ **c. garlic leaves** (if you do not grow garlic in your garden, substitute **2 cloves** of **garlic),** and **grated rind** of **1 lemon.**

6) Cook **1 lb. pasta** of your choice. Linguine would be a good selection. Drain pasta and return to cooking pot. Add as much sauce as seems necessary. Heat briefly, and toss in a generous amount of gremolata.

7) Garnish with toasted pignoli nuts and **Parmesan cheese.** Offer extra gremolata on the side.

Serves 4 with sauce left over

The concept of 'appropriate technology' refers to a lifestyle that many women have always lived. The constant recycling of scarce resources, of garbage saved for gardens and cloth scraps used for quilts, has been an ongoing part of most women's lives. Whether because they have had little access to other resources, or because they are more respectful of the need to give back to nature what they have taken, women have more consistently seen resources as non-renewable.

Woman's Worth
Lisa Leghorn and Katherine Parker;
Routledge and Kegan Paul

SPRING THALI

Less elaborate than the Winter Thali, this party platter is still a lot of work. Consider making just one of the vegetable dishes, either **Dum Aloo** (potatoes cooked with yoghurt), **Mattar Panir** (peas), or **Gobhi Subzi** (cauliflower) to serve with **Basmati Rice** and **Dahl**, and possibly **Raita** for a simpler dinner. We find the rice and dahl satisfying all by themselves.

To do the Spring Thali as we serve it, make basmati rice, dahl, and raita (see recipe index). Center rice on thali platter and pour dahl gravy over it. Place bowls of dum aloo, gobhi subzi, mattar panir, and raita around the rice. A small piece of **Lime Pickle** and **Mint Chutney** complete the meal. You can even serve **Kheer** (Indian rice pudding) for dessert.

Hecate is called the Goddess of crossroads, i.e. choices. I must choose which of the lettuces to pull, which to leave. I wield the terrible power that I, as an infant, attributed to my mother: the power to annihilate. I can, I must, choose that power again and again; for every choice I take annihilates some other possibility.

Dreaming the Dark
Starhawk; Beacon Press

DUM ALOO

Potatoes cooked in a yoghurt sauce.

1) Wash **1 ½ lb. small new potatoes** (or cut up larger ones into big chunks) and peel or not, as you prefer. Pierce each potato in several spots with a skewer. In a frying pan heat **2 Tb. oil** and fry the potatoes over high heat until browned on all sides. Remove to a sauce pot and turn heat off under frying pan.

2) Chop enough **onion** to measure ¾ **c.** and grate ½ **Tb. ginger.** Add to frying pan with more **oil** if necessary and saute with **1 t. coriander seed** and ½ **hot chili pepper,** minced. When vegetables are beginning to brown, turn into pot with potatoes. Add **1 ½ t. salt, pinch cayenne,** ½ **t. cumin, 2 bay leaves,** and ½ **t. tumeric.** Also add **1 c. yoghurt** and turn potatoes in spice mixture. Add a few tablespoons **water** if it seems necessary. Cover and simmer until potatoes are tender, about 20 minutes.

3) Chop **2 Tb. cilantro** and fold into mixture.

Serves 6

MATTAR PANIR

Peas with cheese. We use tofu cubes instead, as
suggested by our friend Swadesh.

1) Dice enough **tofu** in ½" pieces to yield **1 c.** Fry in
   several batches in very hot **oil** or if you prefer,
   clarified butter, until crispy and golden. Remove and
   drain on absorbent paper.

2) Grate **1 Tb. fresh ginger** and finely chop **2
   cloves garlic.** Chop ½ **c. onion.** Add all three to
   frying pan with ½ **t. salt.** Saute until soft and
   beginning to brown. Add ½ **t. tumeric, pinch
   cayenne,** ½ **t. ground coriander,** and **1**½ **t.
   garam masala** (a spice mixture similar to curry
   powder: see recipe index). When well blended, add
   ¾ **c. water** and **1 fresh tomato,** chopped.
   Simmer 5 minutes. Add **4 c. fresh shelled** or
   frozen peas and cook until peas are done.

Serves 6

GOBHI SUBZI

Curried cauliflower.

1) Heat **2 Tb. oil** in a saucepan. Add **1 t. black mustard seed** and ½ **t. whole cumin seed.** Cook 3-4 minutes. Now add **1 Tb.** freshly grated **ginger** and ½ **c.** finely chopped **onions.** Cook another minute or two. Add **1 ½ t. salt, 1 t. tumeric** and let stew 3-4 minutes longer while you prepare the cauliflower.

2) Divide **1 large cauliflower** into flowerets and add to pot, raising heat to high. Turn the pieces in the hot seasoning mixture. When well coated and beginning to brown, add **1 fresh tomato,** chopped, **1** finely minced **hot chili,** and ½ **t. ground cumin.** Cover pot and lower heat to simmer. Cook cauliflower until barely done, turning pieces occasionally. Cooking should not take more then 10 minutes. Garnish with freshly chopped **cilantro.**

Serves 6

MINT CHUTNEY

1) Place in processor: **1½ c. fresh mint leaves, 1** seeded **hot chili, 1½ Tb.** sliced **onion, ½ t.** diced **fresh ginger, ⅓ t. salt, ⅓ t. honey, 1 Tb. lemon juice,** and **½ Tb. water.**

2) Turn processor on and off until chutney is chopped fine. Add **2-3 Tb. plain yoghurt** if you like. Refrigerate and serve with Indian Thali. Chutney does not keep more than a few days.

Yields about 2 cups

There probably is really no distinction, in the end, between imagination and courage. We can't imagine what we can't face, and we can't face what we can't imagine. To break out of the structures of the arrogant eye we have to dare to rely on ourselves to make meaning and we have to imagine ourselves being capable of that: capable of weaving the web of meaning which will hold us in some kind of intelligibility.

The Politics of Reality: Essays in Feminist Theory
Marilyn Frye; Crossing Press

LASSI

A refreshing Indian drink. This recipe is for a salty lassi. Some Indian restaurants serve sweet ones.

1) In a blender combine **1 ½ c. plain yoghurt, 1 ½ c. buttermilk, 1 t. salt, 1 t. ground cumin,** and **1 ½ c. water.** Blend together.

2) Fill 3 large glasses with **ice cubes.** Pour lassi over the ice and serve.

Makes 3 drinks

Among the last active preservers of Goddess-worship in Europe were the gypsies, who began to migrate westward from Hindustan about 1000 A.D. Because Christians identified their beliefs with witchcraft, gypsies were popularly known as Minions of the Moon, or Diana's Foresters . . . Gypsies revered the female principle as the source of life; they said, "For us, woman is like the earth. The earth is our mother, and so is woman. The secret of life comes from the ground."

The Woman's Encyclopedia of Myths and Secrets
Barbara Walker; Harper and Row

KHEER

An Indian milk and rice dessert.

1) Bring **2 qt. milk** to a boil in a large pot. Turn down heat to simmering, stirring off and on for 15 minutes or until milk ceases threatening to boil over.

2) When milk has simmered about 30 minutes, wash **⅓ c. long grain white rice** and add to pot. Simmer another 30 minutes, stirring every 5 minutes.

3) Open **3 whole cardamom pods.** Crush seeds coarsely with a rolling pin. Finely chop **¼ c. almonds.** Add almonds and cardamom seeds to kheer. Stir over low heat for another 25 minutes or until mixture is slightly thickened but still creamy. When refrigerated, kheer will thicken up. Since it is supposed to be quite soft in consistency, don't overcook. Before it is quite done, add **¼ t. salt** and **¼ c. honey.** After removing kheer from heat, add **1 t. rosewater** and stir well. Cool, refrigerate.

4) Serve topped with **toasted slivered almonds** or chopped **pistachio nuts.**

Serves 8

SOY MILK KHEER

A dairy free dessert.

1) Make **soy milk** as described in recipe for Mocha Almond Soy Creme (see recipe index). You will need **2 qts.**

2) Bring soy milk to a simmer in a large pot. Proceed with kheer exactly as in preceeding recipe. The soy milk pudding is indistinguishable from the milk based pudding.

Serves 8

Unable to prevent the irresponsible use of nuclear power, to eliminate poverty and the agony of starving abandoned, deprived and brutalized children, the most radical elements of our society have chosen to defend rapists, pornographers and child molesters.

The Best Kept Secret: Sexual Abuse of Children
Florence Rush; Prentice-Hall, Inc.

GULAB JAMIN

An Indian doughnut.

1) In a small pot simmer **4 Tb. sweet butter** 20-30
   minutes until all milk solids have evaporated and the
   butter is a light, nutty brown. This is "ghee". Cool at
   least 5 minutes.

2) In a food processor combine **1 c. non-fat dry milk,
   ¼ c. flour, ¼ t. baking soda, 1 ½ t. baking
   powder.** Turn processor on and off to mix the dry
   ingredients, and then add **3 Tb. ghee,** mixing the
   same way. Turn processor off. Measure out ½ c.
   milk and turn machine on again. Slowly add milk,
   using just enough to make a stiff but pliable, taffy-like
   dough that is well kneaded. You will use from ⅓ c. to
   ½ c. of milk.

3) Use the remaining **1 Tb. ghee** to moisten your hands
   while you roll 24-25 small balls from the dough mixture
   in the processor. Place in a bowl or on a plate. Set
   aside.

4) In a wide-bottomed, shallow sauce pot combine **1 ½ c.
   honey** and **1 ½ c. water.** Open **3 cardamom
   pods** and add the seeds to the syrup (discard the
   outer shells). Cook syrup 15-20 minutes. If you have
   no cardamom pods, you can add ½ t. **ground
   cardamom** to the cooked syrup.

5) Heat **oil** for deep frying in a pot or wok. Oil should
   not be as hot as for most deep frying. Try frying one
   doughnut. It should sink to the bottom and then
   slowly rise after 10 seconds. If fat is too hot, turn off
   heat and let cool. Add doughnuts when fat seems
   right and fry 5-6 at a time. They will rise and roll over
   prettily to brown themselves on all sides. Drain onto
   absorbent paper and repeat until all are done.

6) Add **1 t. rose water** to honey syrup. Add
   doughnuts to pot with warm syrup, tilting and
   spooning syrup over doughnuts. Do not cook further.

7) Serve warm or at room temperature, 3 to a person,
   with a little syrup in the dish. Finely chopped
   pistachios are a nice garnish.

                                                   Serves 8

*Down in Luzanna, where I grew up, fat on a woman is
a desirable thing. If you're walking down the street and
run into an old friend you haven't seen in years, she'll
most likely say; "Hey Cher, how you been doing? You
gained a little weight I see . . . girl you sho look good."*

What Don't Kill Is Fattening
Luisah Teish; FanTree Press

CARAMEL FLAN

Flan recipes are simple and usual. This one is exceptional, because it is made of egg yolks and is flavored with liqueur.

1) Preheat oven to 350°. In a small pot bring ⅓ **c. water** and ½ **c. sugar** to a boil. Cook over moderate heat until mixture turns an amber brown. Pour into a ring mold, tilting mold so that caramel will coat some of the sides. Be very careful handling the caramel; it can cause bad burns.

2) In another pot bring **6 c. milk** almost to a boil. Meanwhile in a large bowl place **12 egg yolks** plus **2 whole eggs** (save whites for Green Goddess Souffle). Whisk with ¾ **c. sugar, scant** ½ **t. cinnamon, 2 Tb. brandy**, and **2 Tb. creme de cacao.** When well blended, gradually add hot milk, stirring carefully.

3) Ladle mixture into prepared ring mold. Place mold in a larger pan and put into preheated oven. Add enough water to the larger pan to reach half way up the sides of the mold. Bake for about 1 hour or until a toothpick inserted in the center comes out clean. Remove from oven and cool on a rack. Place in refrigerator. When flan is quite cold, turn it out onto a rimmed platter, so that the thin caramel sauce is contained on the dish.

Serves 10-12

FLAN SYLVIA

The variation here is the use of cream cheese for subtly different flavor and texture. From Adelita Chirino.

1) In a small pot bring ⅓ **c. water** and ½ **c. sugar** to a boil and continue to cook over moderate heat until caramel turns amber brown. Pour into a ring mold and tilt to coat part of the sides as well as the bottom. Be very careful handling caramel. Burns from it are serious. Set mold aside. Preheat oven to 350°.

2) In a medium sized pot bring **2 ½ c. milk** and **1 c. heavy cream** to a simmer. Meanwhile use a mixer to cream **4 oz. cream cheese** with ⅓ **c. sugar**. Beat in **6 egg yolks** and **1 whole egg**. Add **dash** of **salt**. Flavor with **2 Tb. Jamaican rum**. Gradually add hot milk, stirring well.

3) Pour or ladle custard into ring mold. Place in a larger pan and put in oven. Add water to outer pan to reach halfway up the sides of the mold. Bake until a toothpick inserted in the center comes out clean, which may take as long as 1 hour. Cool, refrigerate, then run a knife around inner and outer rims. Turn out onto a serving platter.

Serves 6

MAPLE RHUBARB TOFU MOUSSE

An elegant dairy free dessert.

1) In a stainless steel pot mix together **2 Tb. agar-agar flakes** and **2 c. good fruit juice.** (Apple strawberry or apple raspberry from a health food store are preferred.) Bring to a simmer, add **1 cake tofu** (8 oz.) and cook gently 10 minutes. Lift tofu out and set it and the liquid aside.

2) Pulverize ¾ **c. sunflower seeds** or a mixture of **dried coconut** and **walnuts** very finely in a small coffee mill or food processor. Now use processor to combine the finely ground seeds or nuts with ⅓ **c. maple syrup,** adding ¾ **c. oil** very slowly, alternately with pieces of the drained tofu. The mixture should thicken like a mayonnaise if oil is added slowly enough. When well mixed and smooth, scrape down, add **1 t. lemon juice,** ¾ **t. salt,** and **1 t. vanilla extract.** Turn machine on again and add the agar-agar and juice to the mixture. Taste for salt and sweet.

3) Lightly oil a ring mold or 7 individual custard cups or tea cups. Agar-agar does not make as stiff a mousse as gelatin would, so you cannot use a tall peaked mold. Individual molds work quite well, however. Fill molds and refrigerate.

4) Dice **2 c. rhubarb** and put into a pot with ¼ c. **maple syrup** and ¼ c. **apple strawberry juice.** Let stand half hour and then simmer until rhubarb is done, about 15 minutes. Cool, refrigerate.

5) Use a knife to loosen edges of mousse. Turn out ring mold onto a serving plate or turn out individual molds onto saucers. Top with rhubarb sauce.

Serves 7

When we talk of a female future we are talking of something that once existed and that has been deliberately and with full malice held down and controlled by means so violent that no nonaggressive entity could hope to resist. We are talking here about the power of women, felt by every woman at some time in her life, that tremendously rich and life-giving, life-affirming force . . . Even though we can't know that a female future would save the world, we have nothing to lose from acting as if it would.

"The Future — If There Is One — Is Female"
Sally Miller Gearhart
Reweaving the Web of Life: Feminism and Nonviolence
Ed: Pam McAllister; New Society

~~~~~~

CHAPTER 4   SUMMER

One other discipline is essential both to the practice of
feminism and to its theoretical integrity: the firm,
unsentimental, continuous recognition that women are a
class having a common condition . . . This definition
cannot exclude prudes or sluts or dykes or mothers or
virgins because one does not want to be associated with
them . . . There is no real feminism that does not have at
its heart the tempering discipline of sex-consiousness:
knowing that women share a common condition as a
class, like it or not.

Right Wing Women
Andrea Dworkin; Wideview/Perigee

SPINACH SCHAV

To Ashkenazi Jews, schav is sorrel and also the soup made from sorrel. This soup is made with spinach, soured with citric acid (sour salt). It is most refreshing on a hot day. From Frances Zabin.

1) Defrost **2 10 oz. packages** of **frozen chopped spinach.** Put into a stainless steel pot with **2½ c. water, 1 onion,** peeled and cut in half, **1½ t. sour salt,** and **1¼ t. table salt.** Bring to a boil. Soup will turn a yellowish green color.

2) In a medium sized bowl fork beat **2-3 eggs** until frothy. Use a ladle to dip out hot soup into eggs, stirring well so that eggs barely cook but don't curdle. Gradually add all the soup to the eggs. Dilute with **1¾ c. cold water.** Cool and chill in refrigerator.

3) Before serving, taste soup for **salt** and **sour salt.** Dilute with **water** if necessary. Hard boil **2 eggs.**

4) Garnish with **sour cream,** chopped **scallions,** diced **cucumber,** and hard boiled egg slices. To make a meal of this soup, you can also serve boiled **new potatoes** on the side.

Serves 6-7

HUNGARIAN GREEN BEAN
& POTATO SOUP

From Marie Gall.

1) Cut **1 qt. green beans** into 1½" lengths. Put into a
   pot with **2 c. water** and simmer briefly until tender.
   Set aside.

2) Peel and dice **6 medium potatoes** and cook in
   1 c. water until barely done.

3) Chop **1 large onion.** Saute very slowly in **4 Tb.
   butter** and **1 Tb. Hungarian paprika** in a soup
   pot. The good flavor of this soup depends on the
   quality of paprika used. Purchase paprika either
   loose ("medium sharp rose") or in cans ("Szeged")
   from Hungarian or Eastern European grocery
   stores.   When onions begin to brown, add ¼ **c.
   flour** and continue sauteeing, stirring, for 5-10
   minutes more.

4) Pour liquids from beans and potatoes into onion roux
   and whisk together well. Add **2⅔ c. milk,** ¼ **c. shoyu,**
   freshly ground **pepper, 3 Tb. cider vinegar.** If
   you have **fresh dill** and **fresh summer savory,**
   chop **1 Tb.** of each and add to soup. Add beans and
   potatoes and reheat. Taste to see if any **salt** or more
   vinegar is needed.

5) This refreshing summer soup tastes fine as is, but
   may be garnished with **sour cream** if you like.

Serves 6-8

KOHLRABI AVGOLEMONO SOUP

This recipe uses a traditional Greek soup as a base for fresh kohlrabi.

1) Peel bulbs of **2 lb. kohlrabi,** saving nice young leaves. Slice bulbs. Bring **5 ½ c. water** to a boil in a soup pot. Add **1 ½ t. salt** and kohlrabi slices. Simmer 10 minutes. Using a slotted spoon, drain slices on paper towelling. Pat dry. Add sliced kohlrabi leaves to broth and simmer about 5 minutes.

2) Heat **4 Tb. sweet butter** in a frying pan, and saute cooked kohlrabi until well browned, doing several batches if necessary. Return browned slices to the soup pot.

3) Make the avgolemono seasoning: In a bowl, whisk together **3 egg yolks** and **1 ½ Tb. lemon juice.** Add a dipper of hot broth, and continue mixing. Melt **8 Tb. sweet butter** in the same frying pan over low heat, and add avgolemono, stirring constantly to slightly thicken mixture. Turn into soup kettle and heat gently.

4) Judge thickness of soup. It may need an additional **2 c. water.** Add **1 ½-2 Tb. shoyu** and freshly ground **pepper.** Correct seasoning. You may want to add another **Tb. lemon juice.** If you grow **summer savory,** chop **1 Tb.** and stir into the soup. Reheat carefully.

Serves 6-7

SANCOCHO

This is a soup-stew to be found in many Caribbean and Latin American countries. It is usually garnished with pork; we substitute frozen tofu. You will find the root vegetables and seasonings in Hispanic markets.

1) A day or so before you want to make Sancocho, freeze **1 lb. tofu** wrapped in foil. Defrost it before you begin to make the soup. Sometimes we find ourselves with more tofu than we can use fresh, and we freeze it in separate blocks, so it is always available for this kind of soup garnish.

2) Make **sofrito** (seasoning base for soup): Gently heat a **few achiote seeds** in ¼ **c. oil** until yellow color is suffused into the oil. Scoop seeds out and discard. Dice **2 green peppers, ½ small jalapeno pepper,** and **1 large onion.** Finely chop **2 cloves garlic** and saute with other vegetables in the yellow oil with **2 t. oregano** and **1 Tb. ground cumin** until vegetables begin to brown. Set frying pan aside.

3) Set a large soup pot on the stove and put **1½ c. water** and **1 c. white rice** into it. Cook gently until rice is done. Turn heat off. Meanwhile, use smaller pot to separately cook the following vegetables. First peel and slice **1 medium yucca,** barely cover with **water** and simmer until tender. Turn into soup pot with cooking liquid. Repeat with **1 small yautia, 2 carrots, 1 yam, 1 batata,** and **1 green plantain.** Unless you know the cooking

time of these vegetables, it is best to cook them individually, preparing each as the last one is done. Peel and cut into chunks ½ **small calabeza** and cook. Husk and cut **2 ears** of **fresh corn** into 2" lengths and steam until just done. Add to soup pot.

4) Dice the tofu into ½" pieces and fry until crispy in the sofrito. Turn sofrito into soup pot and add **1 ripe plaintain,** peeled and sliced, ⅓ **c. shoyu,** and **2 t. salt.** Bring to a simmer and taste for seasoning. Add **water** if necessary.

5) Serve hot, garnished with slices of **avocado** and freshly chopped **cilantro.**

Serves 8

Miss Ruthie made her living by going to the market at Black River every Saturday and selling some of the crops she raised on the quarter-acre she borrowed from Miss Mattie, and the pink-edged coconut cakes and dark brown tamarind balls she made on Friday night. Sometimes she and her daughters gathered cashews from the two trees near the house, blanched and roasted them, and added them to the long deep basket she carried with her. Mostly, she sold callaloo, tomatoes, oranges, mangoes, yam, and cassava.

Abeng
Michelle Cliff; Crossing Press

TEMPEH "CHICKEN" SALAD

1) Steam **1 cake tempeh** (8 oz.) over boiling water for
   20 minutes. Remove to shallow pan. Combine
   2 ½ Tb. white wine and **1 Tb. shoyu.** Pour over
   tempeh and chill one hour.

2) Dice ⅞ **c. hearts** and **inner leaves celery,** ½ **c.**
   green pepper. Finely mince **1 Tb. onion.** Cut
   tempeh into ⅜" dice. Halve and seed ⅔ **c. red grapes**
   and finely chop **2 Tb. straight leaf parsley.**
   Combine in a bowl with any remaining marinade.

3) Use a food processor or a mixer to make
   Mayonnaise: Place **2 small egg yolks** in bowl, add
   1 scant Tb. lemon juice, ¼ **t. salt,** ½ **Tb. dijon**
   mustard, 1 clove garlic, crushed, and start
   machine. Add ⅔ **c. good salad oil,** drop by drop, until
   quite thick and creamy. Turn into bowl with tempeh;
   season with freshly ground **pepper.** Taste for
   lemon juice and **salt.** Chill.

4) Sliver and toast ½ **c. almonds.** Serve salad in
   avocado halves topped with almonds.

Serves 4 generously

TOFU EGGLESS SALAD

1) In a pot cover **2 lb. tofu** with **water** and bring to a boil. Drain on paper towels and press with a lightly weighted tray for 10 minutes. Set aside ½ lb. drained and pressed tofu for the "whites".

2) Dice **2 stalks celery** with **leaves.** Finely chop **1 Tb. chives** or **garlic leaves** and **2 Tb. parsley.**

3) Place in a bowl or in a food processor 1½ lb. of the tofu, broken into large pieces, and the chopped vegetables. Add ¼ **c. oil,** ¼ **t. tumeric,** ¼ **t. cumin, scant** ¼ **c. shoyu, 1 Tb. nutritional yeast, 1 Tb. lemon juice, 2 Tb. sunflower seeds,** and freshly ground **pepper** to taste. Mash all ingredients together by hand with a potato masher or turn the machine on and off quickly two or three times. The resulting salad should be well mixed with a somewhat lumpy texture like egg salad. Cut the remaining ½ lb. tofu into small pieces and fold it in. Taste for salt, lemon. Add **dash** of **Tabasco** if desired.

4) Serve on a bed of **Boston lettuce** with **new pickle** and **avocado slices** for garnish. Top with **alfalfa sprouts** or thinly sliced **onion** and a **sprinkling** of **gomahsio. Whole wheat toast** is a good accompaniment for this salad.

Serves 4-6

SABRA SALAD

From Batya Bauman.

1) Dice **2 c. fresh, local vine ripened tomatoes.**
   Dice **1½ c. thin, unwaxed cucumbers;** if you
   don't grow your own, use Kirbys. Thinly slice **2-3
   scallions.** Finely chop ¼ c. **straight leaf
   parsley.** Combine in a bowl. Drizzle with **olive oil,**
   and squeeze the **juice** of ½ **lemon** over all. Add
   salt and **pepper** to taste.

2) In a small bowl stir ½ **c. tahini** (Sahadi or Joyva are
   preferred) with a spoon, slowly adding **cold water.**
   Tahini will thicken at first. Keep adding water until
   sauce is creamy. Add about **3 Tb. lemon juice, 3
   cloves** crushed **garlic,** and **salt** to taste.

3) Serve salad in individual dishes and let each diner
   add tahini dressing as desired.

Serves 4

STIR FRIED BOK CHOY
WITH MUSHROOMS & TOFU

Bok choy is an easy vegetable to grow, with fine flavor best suited to stir frying.

1) Put up **1 c. short grain brown rice** to cook slowly in **1¾ c. water** and **½ t. salt.** Rice will need about 40 minutes to cook.

2) Soak **2 oz. dried Chinese mushrooms** in **warm water.** Set aside.

3) In a four-cup measure combine **¼ c. shoyu, ¼ c. dry sherry, ¼ c. cornstarch,** and **3 c. water.** Add a **scant ½ t. Chinese chili paste with garlic.** Set aside.

4) Chop **1 large onion.** Mince **2-3 cloves garlic.** Wash and then cut **1½ qt. bok choy** in thin diagonal slices. Lift mushrooms from liquid, squeeze gently and slice, discarding any tough stems. Reserve soaking water.

5) Heat a wok or frying pan and add **2 Tb. oil.** Add onion, bok choy, and mushrooms. Stir fry, lifting and turning vegetables. Add garlic and continue to cook vegetables until softened and golden brown. This will take 10-15 minutes.

6) Stir the shoyu-cornstarch mixture well, adding the reserved mushroom soaking liquid. Pour into hot wok or frying pan and continue stirring until sauce is simmering and thickened.

7) Dice ½ **lb. cake** of **tofu** and add to wok. See if any **salt** is needed. Serve over cooked brown rice. Garnish with chopped **scallions.**

Serves 4

our faces,
strong, brown,
different as
the bumps
on the skin of
bittermelon.
our tongues,
sharp and fragrant
as ginger,
telling our history,
our experiences
as asian american women,
workers and poets,
cutting the ropes
that bind us,
breaking from
the silence of centuries

"It's In The Name"
The Words of a Woman who Breathes Fire
Kitty Tsui; Spinsters, Ink

TEMPEH LETTUCE ROLLS

From Mike Gross.

1) Prepare **Hoisin Coconut Tamarind Sauce** (see following recipe).

2) Cut **1 cake tempeh** (8 oz.) into ½″ dice. Mix together in a small bowl: **3 Tb. shoyu, 2 Tb. dry sherry, ¾ Tb. fresh ginger,** grated, **2 cloves** crushed **garlic, 1½ t. coriander,** and **2 t. salt.** Stir well and add tempeh to marinate for 15 minutes or longer.

3) Soak **6 dried Chinese mushrooms** in **1 c. hot tap water.**

4) You will need **6 c. mung bean sprouts** (if home grown, wash off hulls and dry gently), and **1½ c. water chestnuts,** canned or fresh (preferably). Dice **1 large onion.** In a small bowl fork beat **3 eggs** with **1½ t. dry sherry** and **1½ t. shoyu.** Measure out ⅓ **c. Hoisin sauce** and dilute with ½ **c. water.**

5) Drain soaked mushrooms, reserving liquid. Cut off tough stems and discard. Dice mushrooms.

6) Heat **2 Tb. cooking oil** with **1 Tb. sesame oil** in a frying pan. First stir fry the eggs. When just barely cooked, turn out into a large bowl. Then, adding more **oil** (in the same proportions) when necessary, stir fry bean sprouts, onion, water chestnuts, and mushrooms in several batches. As each is done, turn into bowl with eggs. Finally, heat the pan very hot with a little more **oil** and add the drained tempeh. Stir fry until nicely browned, and turn into same bowl. Turn heat off and let frying pan cool a few seconds. Then add mushroom soaking liquid, diluted Hoisin sauce, and any leftover marinating liquid. Bring to a simmer, scrape up any burnt pieces, and add to bowl. Mix thoroughly. Cover to keep warm until ready to serve or steam to reheat.

7) Wash **3 soft outer leaves** of **Boston lettuce** for each diner. Chill. At dinner time, spoon warm filling into cold lettuce leaves and roll up. Pour warmed Hoisin Coconut Tamarind Sauce over rolls, and garnish each plate with **shredded carrots.**

Serves 6-8

Law, religion, and psychoanalytic theory have the same rules; only their styles of enforcement differ. Law and religion say, "Obey." Psychoanalysis says, "Adjust."

Growing Up Free
Letty Cottin Pogrebin; Bantam

HOISIN COCONUT TAMARIND SAUCE

To serve with Tempeh Lettuce Rolls.

1) Soak **1 c. dried coconut** in **1 c. hot tap water** in a blender for 5 minutes. Blend well; set aside.

2) Soak **1 ½ Tb. tamarind seeds** (available in Asian markets) in ⅓ **c. cold water** for 10 minutes. Meanwhile, grate **1 Tb. fresh ginger** into a saucepot. Add **4 small cloves** crushed **garlic** and **1 Tb. sesame oil.** Saute a few minutes so that garlic and ginger are barely cooked.

3) Add the following to the pot: ¼ **c. dry sherry, 1 ½ t. coriander, 2 t. salt,** ⅓ **c. shoyu,** and ⅔ **c. Hoisin sauce.** Bring to simmer.

4) Rub tamarind pulp off seeds and strain into a bowl. Drain coconut into a sieve, squeeze pulp and discard. Add tamarind and coconut milk to sauce. To thicken sauce, stir together **3 Tb. cornstarch** with ½ **c. water** and add to simmering liquid. If sauce becomes too thick or tastes too strong, dilute with **water.**

Makes 3-4 c. sauce

PENNSYLVANIA DUTCH DINNER

This Pennsylvania Dutch dinner in August features a fresh **Corn Custard,** pickled **Red Beet Eggs, Sweet and Sour Green Beans, Spiced Cantaloupe, Spiced Nuts,** and flaky **Buttermilk Biscuits.**

CORN CUSTARD

1) Use a small, sharp knife to scrape kernels from **12 ears of corn.** You will need about **3 c.** Heat oven to 325°.

2) In a separate bowl beat **6 eggs** until foamy. Finely chop enough **onion** to make **2 Tb.,** and add to eggs. Grate enough **Swiss** or **chedder cheese** to measure ⅔ **c.** and add to eggs, together with **1 t. salt,** ⅓ **c.** chopped **parsley,** ⅔ **c. plain bread crumbs,** ⅔ **c. heavy cream, dash cayenne,** and freshly ground **pepper.**

3) Butter 6-8 oven proof custard cups or use a single mold. Combine corn kernels with custard and turn into mold(s). Set in a baking pan deep enough to add water to come halfway up sides of mold(s). Bake until custard is puffed and brown. Let rest several minutes and then turn out. Leftover individual custards can be reheated in a steamer.

Serves 6

RED BEET EGGS

1) Trim and scrape **2 bunches baby beets.** It is best to use a small, serrated knife. Don't wash the beets; rinse the knife instead. Slice beets and cook in **3 c. water** for 30 minutes.

2) Meanwhile, hard boil **6 eggs** in a separate pot. When done, shell eggs under cold running water.

3) Use a slotted spoon to remove beets from their cooking liquid to a bowl. To the red liquid still in the pot, add ¼ **c. honey,** ½ **c. white vinegar, 1 t. prepared mustard,** and **1 t. salt.** Simmer together about 5 minutes.

4) Return beets to cooking liquid and add the shelled eggs. Bring gently to the boil again, then remove pot from heat and let cool.

5) Thinly slice **1 onion.** If **fresh thyme** or **oregano** is available, chop **2 t.** of either. Add herb and onion to beets and eggs. Chill.

6) To serve, slice eggs in half lengthwise. Arrange beets on a serving dish with egg halves around them.

Serves 6-8

SWEET & SOUR GREEN BEANS

1) Dice **2 medium onions.** Saute in **1½ Tb. oil** with **1 t. dried summer savory** (or **1 Tb. freshly chopped savory**) until transparent and golden. Set aside.

2) Stir together in a bowl: **⅓ c. vinegar, 1 c. dry sherry, 1½ Tb. shoyu, 3 Tb. honey,** and **1 Tb. plus 1 t. cornstarch.** Set aside.

3) Cook **1 qt. fresh string beans** in **¾ c. water** until barely done and still bright green. Quickly add cornstarch mixture and return to boil, stirring. As soon as cornstarch clarifies and bean sauce is thickened, remove from heat. Mix in onions and let cool. Serve at room temperature.

Serves 6-8

After a few moments, Lindy controlled her tears. It disheartened her when she and Neddie were both crying at the same time. She tightened her arm around Neddie and prayed silently for the courage to face their own unchartered aging . . . To open the tightness in her throat, inaudibly against Neddie's breasts she extrapolated the words of her fiftieth birthday toast: I can't believe they're going to let one of us bury the other in peace.

Saturday Night in the Prime of Life
Dodici Azpadu; Aunt Lute Book Company

SPICED CANTALOUPE

If possible, make Spiced Cantaloupe a day or two ahead.

1) Cut up **1 cantaloupe** and remove fruit from rind. Cut into 1" chunks, and turn fruit into jars.

2) In a small pot combine ⅓ **c. honey,** ⅓ **c. water, 3 Tb. white vinegar,** a **2" stick cinnamon,** and **4 cloves.** Bring to a boil and cook, uncovered, 5 minutes. Pour over fruit and refrigerate.

SPICED NUTS

1) Brush a cookie sheet with **butter.**

2) In a small bowl combine ⅓ **c. sugar,** ½ **t. cinnamon,** ¼ **t. cloves,** ⅛ **t. nutmeg,** ⅛ **t. ginger,** ⅛ **t. allspice,** and ¼ **t. salt.** Stir together well. Separately beat **1 egg white** with **1 Tb. water,** then add to the sugar mixture.

3) Dip nuts a few at a time into spice mixture and lay on cookie sheet. We use a combination of ½ **c. almonds,** ½ **c. walnuts,** and ¼ **c. filberts.** Bake at 275° for 30-45 minutes.

BUTTERMILK BISCUITS

1) Use a whisk to stir together **2⅓ c. flour, 1½ Tb. baking powder,** ¾ **t. baking soda,** and ¾ **t. salt.** Use pastry blender to cut in **5½ Tb. sweet butter** until mixture looks like oatmeal flakes. Stir in **1 c. buttermilk.** Mix together briefly and pat out on a floured board. Heat oven to 450°.

2) Use a pastry wheel to cut biscuits into diamond shapes. Prick with floured fork. Bake about 5 minutes, use a pancake turner to flip biscuits over, and bake another 5 minutes, or until light brown on both sides.

3) Serve hot with **butter** and **jam,** preferably **elderberry.** Biscuits can be frozen and reheated.

Makes about 1 dozen

"Everywhere in science the talk is of winners, patents, pressures, money, no money, the rat race, the lot; things that are so completely alien . . . that I no longer know whether I can be classified as a modern scientist or an an example of a beast on the way to extinction."

Barbara McClintock
A Feeling For The Organism: The Life and Work of Barbara McClintock
Evelyn Fox Keller; W. H. Freeman and Co.

PAN GRILLED
JAPANESE BABY EGGPLANT

Simple treatment for home grown vegetables.

1) Cook brown rice to go with the eggplants: Wash **1 c. short grain brown rice** and cover with **1¾ c. water.** Simmer 40 minutes or until done.

2) Prepare **Dashi** (sauce) for eggplant: In a small pot combine **1 c. water, ¼ c. shoyu,** and ¼ c. **sake** or **dry sherry.** Add a piece of washed **kombu** if available. Bring to a simmer, remove from heat.

3) Optionally, if you have access to white miso, you can make a tasty topping for the eggplant. Combine ⅓ **c. white (shiro) miso, 1 Tb. sake, 1 Tb. rice wine vinegar, 1½ t. honey,** and ¼ c. of the dashi (above).

4) Add ½ **t.** freshly grated **ginger root** to the remaining dashi.

5) Slice unpeeled **small, thin eggplants** in half lengthwise. Depending on how small they are, plan for 1 or 2 eggplants per diner. Use a sharp knife to cut cross hatch marks in each eggplant half. Cut deeply but not through the skin. Heat **1 Tb. oil** in a frying pan until very hot. Add eggplants, cut side down, adding only the number which fit in one layer. Lower heat to moderate and cover pan. Cook 3-4 minutes. Turn eggplants over and cook, covered, 3-4 more minutes. Finally, uncover pan and be sure each eggplant half is browned and puffed. Repeat for remaining eggplants.

6) Pour a little dashi over eggplant and top with miso mixture, if you are using it. Serve with brown rice and **Sesame Green Beans** (see following recipe).

Enough sauce for 5-6

SESAME GREEN BEANS

1) Toast ½ **c. sesame seeds** in a heavy, dry frying pan, stirring constantly. Remove to a heat proof bowl.

2) Trim **5 c. green beans** and cut in half. Steam in ½ **c. water** and **1 t. salt** until not quite done.

3) Meanwhile, in a small pot, heat **3 Tb. sake** (or **dry sherry**). Add **1 t. honey** and **2 Tb. shoyu.**

4) Add sauce and sesame seeds to green beans and heat all together.

Serves 5-6

SYRIAN BAKED STUFFED EGGPLANT WITH TEMPEH

The tempeh substitutes for lamb in this simple Syrian casserole, and shoyu takes the place of chicken stock.

1) Stuffing: Horizontally slice **1 cake tempeh** to make 2 thinner layers, then dice very finely. Finely chop **1 medium onion.** Saute both in ⅓ **c. olive oil,** adding ⅔ **c. pignoli nuts, dash ground coriander, dash allspice,** ⅓ **t. nutmeg,** ⅔ **t. cinnamon, salt** and **pepper.** Fry mixture until well browned. Turn off heat, scrape filling into a bowl and deglaze pan with a **splash** of **red wine;** pour into bowl also.

2) Peel **3 medium sized eggplants** and then slice lengthwise into ½″ thick slices. Heat frying pan or griddle very hot and sear eggplant slices on both sides, using little or no **oil.**

3) In a shallow baking pan arrange slices of eggplant side by side, trying to find a matching slice for each one which will sit on top, sandwich style. Spoon about 2-3 Tb. stuffing between the eggplant slices. In a bowl dilute a **29 oz. can plain tomato sauce** with **1 can water,** whisk in ¾ **t. cinnamon, 1 t. salt,** and freshly ground **pepper.** Pour over eggplant sandwiches and bake at 375° for 20 minutes.

4) Meanwhile, prepare **Rice Pilaf:** Finely chop **1
   small onion.** Saute in **2 Tb. olive oil** in frying
   pan with **1 oz.** crushed **Fides** (very fine noodles
   available in Greek stores; sometimes called Shehrieh
   in Arabic stores). Fry until noodles begin to brown.
   Add **2 c. white rice** and saute another 5 minutes,
   stirring well. Stop before noodles burn. Add **3 c.
   water** and **2 Tb. shoyu.** Cover and simmer until
   rice is tender, adding more **water** if necessary.

5) Serve eggplant sandwiches and pilaf with **plain
   yoghurt.**

Serves 8-10

*Elisheva's two string bags bulge with food: hallot and
poppy-seed strudel from the bakery, oranges, bananas,
grapefruits, paper bags of lentils and almonds and
raisins, small eggplants to stuff with tomatoes and
cheese, shiny green and red peppers, squashes,
carrots, turnips. The food she is carrying seems like
parts of women's bodies, assembled in some strange
order . . . Orange breasts and purple thighs protrude
exuberantly in all directions as if about to burst from
the flimsy bags that hold them together.*

The Law of Return
Alice Bloch; Alyson Publications

BAKED SWISS CHARD
WITH MUSHROOMS AND
RICOTTA

1) Thoroughly wash **3 lbs. Swiss chard** or **beet greens.**
Parboil in liquid that clings to leaves. Drain well,
reserving broth for Mornay Sauce. Chop finely and
turn into a bowl.

2) Thinly slice **1½ lbs. mushrooms.** Finely chop
3 cloves garlic and **1½ medium onions.** Saute all 3
vegetables in a frying pan wth **4 Tb. sweet butter**
and **2 Tb. oil** until mushrooms begin to brown. Add
to chard with **1½ c. ricotta cheese,** ½ **c. grated
Parmesan cheese,** and **salt** to taste. Cool.

3) Oil a 9″ x 13″ pan and sprinkle with **bread
crumbs.** Add **4 eggs** and **4 yolks** to cooled
vegetables. Stir well and taste for seasoning. Turn
mixture into pan, smoothing the surface with a
spoon or spatula. Top with **bread crumbs** and
Parmesan cheese, then drizzle lightly with **olive
oil.** Bake at 375° until puffed and crisp on top.

4) Meanwhile, prepare **Mornay Sauce, Rice Pilaf**
(see following recipes), and **Grilled Tomatoes:**
Slice **4 medium tomatoes** in half crosswise and
salt lightly. Sprinkle cut halves with **bread
crumbs, Parmesan cheese,** a little **dried
oregano,** finely chopped **garlic,** and **fresh basil**
(or **pesto,** if available). Dot with **butter.** Just
before serving the Swiss chard, broil tomatoes briefly
until toasted and sizzling brown.

5) Serve the baked Swiss chard with rice pilaf. Spoon
   Mornay Sauce over each serving, and place a broiled
   tomato half on each plate.

Serves 8

you go down to the garden to pick chard
while the strength is in the leaves
crimson stems veining upward into the green
How you have given back to me
my dream of a common language
my solitude of self.
I slice the beetroots to the core,
each one contains a different landscape
of bloodlight filaments, distinct rose-purple
striations like the oldest
strata of the Southwestern canyon
an undiscovered planet laid open in the lens

"Culture and Anarchy"
A Wild Patience Has Taken Me This Far
Adrienne Rich; W.W. Norton

MORNAY SAUCE
FOR SWISS CHARD DINNER

1) In a sauce pot melt **4 Tb. sweet butter** and add
   ¼ c. flour. Cook together a few minutes, stirring
   constantly. Add **1 c. half and half** (light cream)
   and bring to a simmer.

2) Add up to **2 c. reserved broth** from the Swiss chard.
   Dice **¾ c. cheese** (we use Havarti) and add to sauce.
   Simmer until thickened and smooth, stirring with a
   whisk.

3) Season with **1-2 t. lemon juice,** a **few drops
   Tabasco,** **¼ t. salt,** and a **dash** of **shoyu.**

Makes about 1 quart

No hubby, no house, no car, no kid,
no regrets for what I didn't or I did.
I'm settled.

"I'm Settled"
Marcia Deihl
Strong Singers
Cathy Winter and Betsy Rose; Origami Enterprises

RICE PILAF

1) Finely chop **1 small onion** and fry in **3 Tb. olive oil,** along with ½ **c. very fine noodles,** crumbled (we use thin Greek noodles called Fides, available in Middle Eastern markets). After a few minutes, add ½ **c. pignoli nuts.** Continue frying a few more minutes, then add **2 c. white rice** and fry until rice is opaque and noodles are brown.

2) Add ¼ **c. currants, 1½ Tb. shoyu, 3½ c. water,** and ½ **t. salt.** Cover and cook over low heat until rice is tender. Add more **water** if necessary, and taste for **salt** before serving.

Serves 6-8

These winds birth reveling energies
No one can leash.
Let's dare, then, to feel at one with them —
Turn about, too, in the dark,
Spread out our hands and stir the night air —
Musing, as we do, on all that needs disturbing. . .

Gathering within the gathering storm our own force.

We Are All Part Of One Another
Barbara Deming; Ed: Jane Meyerding
New Society Publishers

BLUEBERRY TOFU MOUSSE

A rich, dairy free dessert.

1) In a saucepan combine **1¾ c. apple raspberry juice,
   1¾ c. fresh blueberries,** and **½ lb. tofu.**
   Sprinkle **2½ Tb. agar-agar** over the top and bring
   to a simmer, then cook 5-10 minutes.

2) Meanwhile use a powerful blender or food processor
   to crush ¾ c. mixed **walnuts** and **filberts.** Add ⅓
   c. maple syrup, ¾ **c. oil, 1 Tb. lemon juice, 1
   t. salt,** and **1 t. vanilla extract.** The smoothness
   of this mousse depends on how finely you are able to
   pulverize the nuts.

3) Add tofu, blueberries, and juice to mixture, and
   continue pulverizing as thoroughly as possible. Taste
   for **lemon juice** and for sweetness. Correct
   seasoning.

4) Oil 8 tea cups or custard molds. Pour mousse into
   molds. Cool, refrigerate.

5) Use the same pot to simmer ¾ **c. blueberries** in
   ⅓ **c. apple raspberry juice** and **2 Tb. maple
   syrup.** In a measuring cup stir together ¾ **Tb.
   potato starch** and ¼ **c. juice.** Add to simmering
   sauce, stirring until thickened and clear. Thin, if
   necessary, with more juice. Cool, refrigerate.

6) To serve, run a knife around sides of molds. Turn
   out onto plates and top with blueberry sauce.

Serves 8

*I realized one day after another nuclear protest,
another proposed bill to make a nuclear waste disposal
here, that I had no power with those   My power rests
with a greater being, a silence which goes on behind
the uproar   I decided that in a nuclear holocaust, for
certainly they will be stupid enough to cause one if their
history is any example, that I wanted to be planting
corn & squash . . . When we are gone, someone else
will come   Dinosaur eggs might hatch in the intense
heat of nuclear explosions   I will be sad to see the
trees & birds on fire   Surely they are innocent as none
of us has been
With their songs, they know the sacred   I am in a
circle with that soft, enduring word   In it is the wisdom
of all peoples   Without a deep, deep understanding of
the sacredness of life, the fragility of each breath, we
are lost   The holocaust has already occurred   What
follows is only the burning brush   How my heart aches
& cries to write these words   I am not as calmly
indifferent as I sound I will be screaming no no no
more destruction in that last blinding light*

"No Rock Scorns Me as Whore"
Chrystos
This Bridge Called My Back: Writings By
Radical Women Of Color
Ed: Cherríe Moraga and Gloria Anzaldúa;
Kitchen Table Press

BLUEBERRY ALMOND TOFU "CHEESE" PIE

This dairy free cheesecake rivals cream cheese cakes in flavor, but requires time and careful attention. This is our most requested recipe.

1) Make **Crust:** Preheat oven to 350°. In a food processor chop ¾ **c. almonds.** Turn into bowl. In processor combine ⅓ **c. oil,** ⅓ **c. maple syrup,** ¾ **t. vanilla,** ¼ **t. almond extract,** ½ **c. + 2 Tb. whole wheat flour,** ⅓ **t. baking powder** and ⅓ **t. cinnamon.** Turn machine on and off to combine. Return almonds to processor with **2 Tb. water** and mix until just blended.

2) Oil a 9″ x 12″ baking pan and use a metal spatula to spread crust over bottom. Bake until light brown and slightly withdrawn from the edges. Wash processor.

3) Put ½ **lb. tofu** and 1½ **c. juice (apple apricot or apple raspberry)** in a pot, sprinkle in 1½ **Tb. agar-agar,** and bring to a simmer. Cook gently about 10 minutes. Set juice aside. Lift tofu out to drain in a dish.

4) If available, use a coffee mill to very finely pulverize
²/₃ **c. almonds** and ¹/₃ **c.** each **walnuts** and
filberts. Or pulverize in washed and dried
processor. Whichever machine is used for the initial
operation, the finely ground nuts should end up in
the processor. Add the grated **rind** of **1¹/₂ lemons**
to the machine. Turn on processor and very slowly
add **1¹/₂ c. oil,** drop by drop, alternately with the
drained tofu and **3¹/₂ Tb. lemon juice.** Mixture
should become thick and creamy like a mayonnaise.
If you have added the oil too quickly, it may
separate. If this happens, pour off the oil, turn
machine on, and very slowly add oil again. Flavor
with **1 t. salt, 1 Tb. vanilla,** and ¹/₃ **c. maple
syrup.** Scrape down and mix again. While machine
is running, pour in the juice and agar-agar mixture.
Turn this filling onto the almond crust, spreading
evenly.

5) Rinse pot. Add **1 pt. blueberries,** ²/₃ **c. apple
raspberry juice,** ¹/₄ **c. maple syrup,** ¹/₄ **t.
cinnamon,** and bring to a boil. Meanwhile, stir
together **1¹/₄ Tb. arrowroot** in ¹/₂ **c. apple
raspberry juice,** stir into simmering blueberry
mixture until thickened, remove from heat and
spoon carefully over pie. Cool and then refrigerate.

Serves 12

RASPBERRY MOUSSE PIE

You have to have a plethora of your own raspberries to want to puree and sieve them, but if you do, this makes a heavenly pie. Sugar free.

1) Use a food processor to pulverize **3 c. raspberries.** Set aside an **additional 1½ c.** of the **best berries** for garnishing the pie. Turn pureed berries into a sieve over a 4-cup measure. You will need 2 c. puree without pips. To make up the right amount, you can add a little **apple raspberry juice.**

2) In a pot combine ½ **c. water,** raspberry puree, and enough **maple syrup** to sweeten. (Sweet varieties of raspberries such as "Brandywine" won't require more than 2 Tb.; "Latham" will require double that amount.) Sprinkle **4 Tb. agar-agar** over puree and bring slowly to a boil. Simmer about 10-15 minutes to completely dissolve agar-agar. Cool and place in refrigerator to chill.

3) Roll out **Pie Crust** (see recipe index), prick bottom, and use foil plus beans to weight crust. Bake at 375° until edges begin to brown. Remove foil and beans, and let crust finish baking. Remove from oven; cool.

4) Beat **1 c. heavy cream** with **2 Tb. kirsch** until stiff. Fold into cooled raspberry agar-agar mixture. Turn into baked pie shell. Arrange reserved berries on top and refrigerate.

Serves 10-12

RASPBERRY CREAM PIE

You don't have to crush the raspberries for this recipe.

1) Preheat oven to 375°. Make **Pie Crust** (see recipe index) to line a pie pan. Prick rim, line with foil, and weight with dried beans. Bake until edges begin to brown. Remove foil and beans, and finish baking.

2) Heat ½ **small jar** of **raspberry preserves** in a small pot, simmering 5 minutes. Use a brush to coat bottom of pie crust with this glaze, which also serves as a waterproofing measure.

3) Scald **1¾ c. milk.** In a bowl beat **7 egg yolks** until light and fluffy. Add ⅓ **c. sugar** and continue beating. Add ¼ **c. unbleached white flour** and a **pinch salt.** Add milk gradually to egg mixture, stirring constantly. Return to pot and cook very slowly until mixture thickens, using a whisk to reach all corners of the pot. When thickened, flavor with **2 Tb. kirsch.** Let cool slightly. Pour into baked pie shell.

4) Cover top of pie with **fresh raspberries.** (You will need about **3 c.** to cover a 10″ pie.)

5) Before serving, beat **2 c. heavy cream** with **2 Tb. kirsh** until stiff. Serve on top of pie.

Serves 12

PLUM UPSIDE DOWN CAKE

1) Preheat oven to 375°. Remove ½ **c. sweet butter** from refrigerator to soften.

2) Place a 9″ round cake pan on a top burner of the stove. Melt **2 Tb. sweet butter** in pan and then tilt it to butter the sides as well as the bottom. Sprinkle ½ **c. brown sugar** evenly over the butter.

3) Slice 3-4 **ripe plums** (unpeeled) to cover bottom of prepared pan. The half moon shapes of the plum slices lend themselves to creative spiral patterning.

4) In a medium sized bowl use a dry whisk to blend together **1½ c. flour, 1½ t. baking powder,** and ¼ **t. salt.**

5) In another bowl use your clean hands to cream together softened butter while gradually adding **1 c. sugar.** When sugar no longer feels grainy to the touch, wash your hands and use a wooden spoon to beat **2 eggs** into the mixture, one at a time. Beat well with wooden spoon until well mixed.

6) Measure out ½ **c. milk.** Add ¾ **t. vanilla extract.** Alternately add flour mixture and milk to batter, beginning and ending with flour. Stir only enough to blend; do not overmix. Turn batter into plum-prepared pan. Bang pan once on counter to eliminate large air bubbles.

7) Bake at 375° until sides of cake have shrunk slightly
   from sides of pan and cake is golden brown, about 45
   minutes. Cool 5 minutes on a rack. Run knife around
   rim and turn cake out onto a plate. If you like, make
   whipped cream: Beat **2 c. heavy cream** with **2
   Tb. Japanese Plum Wine** until cream is stiff.
   Serve on top of plum cake.

Serves 10

I have seen lesbian plums which cling to each other
in the tightest of monogamous love
and I have watched lesbian pumpkins
declare the whole patch their playground
profligate & dusky
their voices arouse something in us
which is laughing

ah, everything is lesbian which loves itself

"The Lesbian Bears"
Martha Courtot
New Lesbian Writing
Ed: Margaret Cruikshank; Grey Fox Press

FROZEN ALMOND MOCHA
SOY CREME

Expensive and time-consuming to make, this dairy free
ice cream tastes better than most commercial versions
on the market.

1) You will need **1 qt. soy milk.** It is easiest to
purchase it if you are near a tofu dairy. Or you can
make it yourself. However, use of flavored soy milk
intended for drinking purposes may not work in this
recipe. To make soy milk, add ¾ **c. soy beans** to
3 c. boiling water. Remove from heat, cover pot,
and let stand 12 hours. Drain beans in a colander and
rinse. To get soy milk, bring a pot of about **6 c.
water** to a boil. You will make the soy milk in
several batches. Add 1 c. of soaked soybeans and
2 c. boiling water to a blender and pulverize for
about a minute. Pour into cheesecloth over a
colander in a bowl and squeeze out soy milk. Turn
soybean pulp (okara) into another container and
repeat until all the soybeans are used, mesuring out
2 c. boiling water for each 1 c. of soybeans. When
you are done, simmer soy milk over low heat for
about 15 minutes. Save okara for **Soysage** (see recipe
index). It can be frozen.

2) Add 3½ **Tb. Cafix, 1 Tb. roasted carob,** and a
pinch cinnamon to soy milk. When these dissolve,
remove from heat. Add 1¼ **t. almond extract,
1 Tb. vanilla extract,** and ⅞ **c. maple syrup.**

3) Pulverize **1 c. almonds,** using a coffee mill or good quality food processor. The smoothness of this frozen soy creme depends on how finely the nuts are ground. Put ground nuts in processor and turn machine on. Slowly add **1½ c. oil** and ½ **lb. tofu.** Flavor with **2 Tb. white miso** (or ¾ **t. salt**). When mixture thickens and is like mayonnaise, add soy milk. If mixture is not as smooth as you would like, try using a blender to make it smoother. Chill.

4) Turn into an ice cream maker. When creme is almost frozen, you can fold in ¾ **c.** slivered and toasted **almonds,** if you like. Store in freezer.

5) To make **Fudge Sauce** for the frozen creme: Combine **2 c. water, 4 Tb. Cafix, 2 Tb. carob, 1 Tb. white miso,** and **2 Tb. maple syrup** in a pot. Bring to a boil. Stir together ¼ **c. water** and **2 Tb. potato starch.** Add to pot, stirring until sauce thickens. Flavor with ¾ **t. vanilla extract.**

6) To serve, dip out soy creme onto a split **banana,** top with fudge sauce and toasted **almonds.**

Makes about 1½ qt. soy creme

BEACH PLUM CRUMB PIE

Some years our beach plum trees yield more fruit than we can pick for soup, jam, or puddings. So we make this pie.

1) Stew about **3½ c. whole beach plums** in a **few Tb. water,** covered, until soft. Push through a colander, discarding pits. You will need **2¼ c. puree.**

2) Preheat oven to 400°. Roll out **Pie Crust** (see recipe index) and fit into pan. Prick bottom, weight wth foil and dried beans. Bake 5 minutes. Remove foil and beans, and take partially baked crust from oven. Set aside, leaving oven on.

3) In a stainless steel pot combine **3 Tb. arrowroot** with **3 Tb. water.** Mix to a paste. Add ⅓ **c. maple syrup.** Add reserved beach plum puree and bring to a boil, stirring well with a wooden spoon. Let bubble 30 seconds after it boils, still stirring, then turn off heat. Remove from burner.

4) Make crumb topping: Use your fingers to rub together ¼ **c. sweet butter,** ⅓ **c. date sugar** (available at health food stores), **1 c. flour,** and a **pinch salt.** Set aside.

5) Use a small knife to cut pits from **whole beach plums.** You will need **1½ c.** of these. Strew over prebaked crust. Place in oven and ladle thickened puree on top. Sprinkle crumbs over all. Bake 40-45 minutes until crisped and bubbly. A cookie sheet on the oven floor will catch drips. This pie is best served warm. Some will like it with **vanilla ice cream.**

Serves 12

Her younger neighbors think that she is lonely,
that only death keeps her company at meals.
But I know what sufficiency she may possess.
I know what can be gathered from year to year,
gathered from what is near to hand, as I do
elderberries that bend in damp thickets by the road,
gathered and preserved, jars and jars shining
in rows of claret red, made at times with help,
a friend or a lover, but consumed long after,
long after they are gone and I sit
alone at the kitchen table.

"The Sound of One Fork"
Minnie Bruce Pratt
Lesbian Poetry
Ed: Elly Bulkin and Joan Larkin; Persephone Press

CHAPTER 5

BREADS & BREAKFAST

Sister
the rape of a woman
is the rape of the earth
the rape of a child
the rape of the universe . . .
Sister
hear me now
let us take this
journey together.

"this woman that i am becoming"
Marcie Rendon (Awanewquay)
Sinister Wisdom: A Gathering of Spirit
North American Indian Women's Issue

Old Gaya's children stand at the intersections of the universe pointing out the various directions. And the intersection may be a Dianic crossroad where offerings were left, an Indian four-direction cross painted on the ground, a Voodoo or an African cross marked in wood, or an Asian crossroad related in a story. Or the crossroad may be pointed out as a dream of another world, the possibility of going "over the rainbow." In tribal culture we often formed a pool of potential initiates some of whom became the shamans and medicine people who can enter the spirit world, the wind, the mountains and rivers and the bottom of the sea; the worlds of the dead, or spirits, of other people's minds, . . . we it is who bring back the strange and old messages, interpreting them for the benefit of our tribe. . . . What we perhaps have at the core is an uncanny ability to identify with what we are not, to die as one form and return as another, to go from shy cocoon to rampant butterfly, to enter the wolves' den to learn the wolves' wisdom and return uneaten, though not unmarked. We have been the oracles and inspired diviners, the mediums who interpret the stars, the cards. . . . the history and poetry and saga of a people. And we remain remarkably tuned to a particular inner vision that is compelling to us, leading us into sometimes painful, grueling, lonely lives. All the more so when we cannot say our names.

Another Mother Tongue: Gay Words, Gay Worlds
Judy Grahn; Beacon Press

SCRAMBLED TOFU

From Dik Rose of Redwood Valley Soyfoods and Bright Song Tofu.

1) Put **1 ½ lb. tofu** into a pot. Use a fork or potato masher to break up tofu into curds resembling scrambled eggs.

2) In a small bowl combine **3 Tb. nutritional yeast, 3 Tb. white miso,** a **few drops shoyu, 3 Tb. water,** and ¼ **t. tumeric.** These ingredients are essential for the good flavor and color of this dish. Mix well with a spoon and fold into tofu. Cover pot and heat gently until tofu is well warmed. Stir from time to time. If necessary, a few drops of **water** may be added to prevent burning and to keep tofu creamy.

3) Meanwhile, thinly slice **2 Italian peppers, 6 fresh mushrooms,** and **half 1 small onion.** In a frying pan fry the vegetables in **2 Tb. oil** over high heat until nicely browned. **Salt** lightly, turn off fire. If you like, deglaze pan with **1 Tb. tawny port.** Fold cooked vegetables into tofu.

4) Serve with toasted **whole wheat bread** and chopped **straight leaf parsley.**

Serves 4-5

POACHED EGGS WITH
CAPER MISO SAUCE

1) Melt **3 Tb. butter** in a saucepan. Add **4 Tb. flour**
   and cook, stirring, a minute or two. Add **1½ c. water**
   and **1 c. dry white wine.** In a small bowl stir **2 Tb.
   water** into **2 Tb. red** or **brown miso** until mixture
   is smooth. Add to sauce. Drain and chop **2 Tb.**
   bottled **capers** (or well washed salted ones). Add to
   sauce. Stir over heat until thickened and smooth,
   adding more **water** if too thick.

2) Leftover **Polenta** (see recipe index) makes a
   different base for these poached eggs. Coat thin
   pieces of it with **flour** and fry in **oil** or **butter** until
   browned at the edges. Keep warm in the oven. Or
   use traditional **toast** for your poached eggs.

3) In a shallow saucepan bring enough **water** to a boil
   to adequately cover the eggs you will be poaching.
   Don't try to poach more than **4 eggs** at a time. The
   best poached eggs are those which come from free
   running chickens. When water is simmering, turn
   heat down and break eggs into the pot. Cover and
   poach 3 minutes. Drain eggs with slotted spoon
   over absorbent paper. Place on toast or polenta,
   and spoon sauce over top. Garnish with chopped
   straight leaf parsley.

                              Makes about 3 c. sauce

SOYSAGE

A somewhat pungent, Italian style sausage made from
okara (a "waste" by-product of tofu manufacture)
instead of pork. If you make your own tofu, you will
have okara left over. Otherwise, health food stores
that carry fresh tofu in bulk may be able to order some
for you. Okara is estimated to be 15-20 percent
protein. You can store it in a freezer until ready to use.
Then be sure to defrost it completely.

1) Prepare **3-4 empty tin cans,** approximately 3"
   diameter by 4½" high, by removing both ends. Wipe
   with an oiled paper towel, and lightly oil 8 squares of
   aluminum foil to seal top and bottom of each can after
   filling is added. Set aside.

2) Chop very finely: **1 very large onion** and ¼ c.
   straight leaf parsley. Set aside.

3) Combine the following "dry" ingredients in a mixer:
   **4 c. okara, 1 c. whole wheat flour, ¾ c.
   bulgar, 1 c. oat flakes, 1 c. nutritional yeast**
   (available in health food stores), and **¼ c. sesame
   seeds.** Mix well. Add chopped vegetables.

4) With mixer still going, add the following seasonings:
   2 t. freshly ground **black pepper, 2¼ t. chili
   powder, 1 t. red pepper flakes, 1 t. celery
   seed, 1 Tb. oregano, 1½ t. salt, 1½ t. whole
   fennel** (or **anise seed**), **¾ t. ground allspice,** and
   1 Tb. dried sage. Crush **3 cloves garlic** and add.

5) Now add the following "wet" ingredients: ⅓ **c. shoyu, ⅔ c. oil, 1 Tb. vinegar,** and **1½ Tb. honey** (or **barley malt**). Now you can add up to ¾ **c. water,** but do not make mixture too moist. You can test by feeling whether you could shape a pattie from the soysage at this point.

5) When soysage is well blended, use a spoon to pack firmly into prepared cans, covering both ends with oiled foil. Use a steamer or rig a soup kettle with some kind of rack so that soysage can be steamed without standing the cans in water. The rim of a springform pan with a cake rack on top works well if you have the right size pot. Steam soysage 1 hour in the covered pot.

7) Use tongs to remove cans. Cool. Run a knife around sides of each can to turn soysage out. Wrap each cylinder in foil and store in freezer. To cook for breakfast, defrost overnight in refrigerator.

8) When ready to serve, slice cylinder into 6-8 patties. Fry on very hot griddle or in a frying pan, adding just a little **oil.** Brown well on one side and then flip over. Serve with **pancakes** and **syrup;** topped with **ketchup** or **Spanish Sauce** (see *The Political Palate*); or accompanied by **home fried potatoes** and **eggs,** as you like.

Each cylinder makes 6-8 patties

FRUIT COMPOTE FRENCH TOAST

Sweetening free and delicious.

1) You will need leftover **Scandinavian Fruit Soup** (see recipe index) for a sauce. Heat **1 c.** in small pot.

2) Cut **4 slices stale bread,** preferably homemade Oatmeal Sunflower Seed Bread from *The Political Palate.* Cut each slice in half crosswise and place in a shallow pan.

3) Fork beat **3 eggs** until foamy. Add ½ **c. milk.** Pour mixture over bread slices and turn them until all liquid is absorbed.

4) Heat **2 Tb. unsalted butter** in a cast iron skillet. Fry as many pieces of soaked bread at a time as you can, turning each with a spatula until puffed and browned. Serve hot topped with fruit sauce.

Serves 4

. . . she keeps her life in separate kitchen cabinets. In fact she is now a closet kosher since she can pass — indeed have high status — by being vegetarian.

"How A Nice Jewish Girl Like Me Could"
Pauline Bart
Nice Jewish Girls; *Crossing*

LECITHIN OIL

From *Sweet & Natural,* a cookbook of "desserts without sugar, honey, molasses or artificial sweeteners" by Janet Warrington, Crossing Press. This recipe makes an excellent mixture for greasing bread, muffin or cake pans. No flouring is necessary.

1) Use a funnel to pour **2 parts liquid lecithin** and **1 part oil** (soy, sunflower, safflower) into a plastic squeeze bottle. Refrigerate the mixture until ready for use, then let it warm to room temperature. Shake well so that oil and lecithin are thoroughly mixed together. Use sparingly, as a little goes a long way.

She is everywhere. The heavens encircle the planet. Everywhere we go we find Her. The star's wink? It is from Her. The summer breezes? Her eyelashes kissing our cheeks. The moon: Her face in the mirror. Our day's sun: the gift of Her hearth. Wherever we go we find Her; when we look to each other, She looks back.
Two women dance the hillside; they see Her everywhere. She is in the dry grass, and in the cricket, and in the warmer air near the ground, moving up hill. Mimi sees Her in Lucile. Lucile sees Her in Mimi. They both feel Her in their own bodies, rushing through: the transforming flood. She is everywhere now, loose.

The City of Hermits
Gina Covina; Barn Owl Books

FOUR GRAIN FRUIT NUT BREAD

Adapted from a recipe by Anna Kalter and Sara Langen, this interesting bread is sweetening free.

1) Roast **1 c. walnuts** in 350° oven about ½ hour until lightly browned and then chop coarsely.

2) Meanwhile, in a pot combine **1¼ c. oatmeal** with **2½ c. water.** Bring to a boil, remove from heat and let cool.

3) In a mixer mash **1 large ripe banana.** Add cooked oatmeal, **1 c. apple juice,** and ⅔ **c. amasake** (or **1⅔ c. apple juice** if amasake is not readily available). The liquid should be slightly warm so that the yeast can grow. Add **2 Tb. dry yeast** and **1 Tb. salt.** Then gradually mix in **1¼ c. rye flour,** ½ **c. whole wheat flour,** ⅔ **c. cornmeal,** ½ **c.** shredded **coconut,** ⅔ **c.** chopped **figs,** ⅔ **c. chopped dates,** ½ **c. oil** and the roasted walnuts. Finally, add **4-5 c. unbleached white flour.** Knead the dough thoroughly 15 minutes by machine or 20-30 minutes by hand. The dough will be moist and somewhat stiff.

4) Turn out into a bowl and let rise in a cool place for 1½ to 2 hours. We find that a longer first rising in a cool place makes better flavored bread than a shorter rising in a warm spot.

5) Preheat oven to 375°. Oil 2 medium sized bread tins (see recipe for **Lecithin Oil**).

6) Punch the bread down. Form into 2 loaves and let rise again for about 30 minutes.

7) Bake in 375° oven until lightly browned and hollow sounding when rapped. Turn out onto racks to cool.

Makes 2 loaves

My poetry, my poetics and my aesthetics all arise out of this chaotic mix, this primordial soup. Melting pots hold no terrors for me because I am one. But the thing about soup, well prepared, is that no flavor is blurred or destroyed. Rather, each flavor is heightened and enhanced, particularized, by the presence of all the rest. I think poetry is a soup. I think poetry is food. I think a poetics that operates like life engendering cooking operates, with knowledge of good ingredients, concentration, training and real knowledge of food, of mixtures that work and mixtures that don't and above all, of food as nourishment, would be a fine and useful poetics . . .

Language, like a woman, can bring into being what was not in being; it can, like food, transform one set of material into another set of material. I think poetry, properly done, is both mother and food, like being the halfbreed Laguna/Lebanese I am is mother and nourishment of what I write and of what I do.

**Songs From This Earth On Turtle's Back:
Contemporary American Indian Poetry**
*Paula Gunn Allen; Ed. Joseph Bruchac;
Greenfield Review Press*

PEACH PLUM PECAN MUFFINS

1) Preheat oven to 400°. Melt **4 Tb. butter.** Cut **3 plums** into slices, separating fruit from the pits. Set aside. Chop **pecans** to yield ⅞ **c.** Peel **2-3 peaches.** You will need ¾ c. diced and ¾ c. pureed. You can use a food processor to puree peaches, then measure. Set both kinds of peaches aside. Butter a muffin tin, or use **Lecithin Oil** (see recipe index).

2) In a bowl whisk together ¾ c. **whole wheat flour, 1¾ c. unbleached white flour, ½ t. baking soda, 1 Tb. baking powder, ½ t. salt, ½ t. cinnamon,** and ⅔ **c. sugar.**

3) In a processor (or mixer) beat **2 eggs.** Add **1 c. buttermilk,** then pour in melted butter and pureed peaches. Turn this wet mixture into bowl with dry ingredients, adding diced peaches and pecans. Fold gently together and spoon into muffin tin. Top each muffin with plum slices. Bake about 25 minutes or until puffed and brown.

Yields 12 muffins

PEAR MUFFINS

1) Preheat oven to 425°. Grease muffin tins with butter or **Lecithin Oil** (see recipe index).

2) Melt ½ **stick sweet butter.** Peel, core, and dice **1½ c. pears.** Set aside.

3) Use a whisk to stir together **2 c. unbleached white flour, 4 t. baking powder, ¼ t. baking soda, ½ t. salt, ½ c. plus 2 Tb. sugar, ½ t. cinnamon, ¼ t. nutmeg,** and a **pinch** of **ginger.**

4) Beat **2 eggs.** Stir in **1 c. sour cream** and the melted butter.

5) Combine wet and dry ingredients with diced pears, taking care not to overmix. Spoon batter into prepared tins and bake at 425° for about 20 minutes. These muffins can be frozen and then reheated in a 350° oven.

Yields 12 muffins

FRUIT NUT KUCHEN

A dairy and sweetening free coffee bread.

1) Simmer **4 c. dried apricots** in **3 c. apple juice** until very soft. Use a processor or blender to puree. Add more juice if necessary to make this a thin mixture for sweetening the bread.

2) Prepare fruit filling and topping: Finely dice ¾ c. **dried dates, 1¾ c. dried apples, ⅓ c. dried pears.** Combine with ⅓ **c. raisins** and ½ c. **currants.** Add ½ t. **cinnamon.** Roast ½ c. **walnuts** and ½ c. **almonds** in 375° oven for 10 minutes; cool and chop. Mix nuts together with fruits and set aside.

3) Bring **2½ c. water** to a boil. Add **1¼ c. oat flakes.** Let cool.

4) In a mixer mash **1 large banana,** add cooled oats, **1⅔ c. amasake** (or **apple juice**), **2 Tb. dry yeast, 1 Tb. salt,** ½ c. **unsweetened dry coconut,** and ⅔ c. finely chopped **dried figs.** Add ½ c. **oil** and **6-7 c. unbleached white flour.** Mix well, using machine, or knead by hand. Turn into a bowl and cover with a towel.

5) Set bread in a cool place for 1½ to 2 hours.

6) When well risen, turn bread out onto a floured counter. Divide into 2 parts. Roll each into a large rectangle. Brush generously with **oil,** then spread even more generously with the apricot puree. Reserve ½ c. for a glaze. You may not need it all. Sprinkle with the chopped dried fruits and nuts, reserving ½ c. for the topping. Roll coffee cake up jelly roll style, then shape into a coil. Let rise 30-45 minutes on an oiled cookie sheet.

7) Bake at 375° until bread is puffed and firm, but not browned. Paint tops with reserved apricot puree and sprinkle with reserved fruit and nuts. Bake until bread is well browned and topping smells good but has not burned. This coffee bread tastes best warm, and individual pieces can be reheated.

Makes 2 loaves or rounds

"Women are bringing the pieces of the truth together. Women are believing again that we have a right to be whole. Scattered pieces from the black sisters, from the yellow sisters, from the white sisters, are coming together, trying to form a whole, and it can't form without the pieces we have saved and cherished. Without the truth we have protected, women won't have the weapons of defense they need. If we hold our secrets to ourselves any longer, we help the evil ones destroy the Womanspirit."

Daughters of Copperwoman
Anne Cameron; Press Gang

A WITCH RECIPE FOR GRIEVERS

Sometimes nothing can be done to change things, and hurt and anger must be transmuted: Examples include the death of someone loved, permanent body damage like breast cancer, dissolution of relationship. See what you can use from this "recipe".

1) In the middle of the worst pain, try to find something to make, to create for yourself. Something difficult and particularly rewarding. Even if you can't start it now, plan to start it soon. Something that will last. Write something, sew something. Use your own special, already polished skill to plan and create a lasting present for yourself. Women used to make mourning quilts and embroideries. (See Judy Chicago's *Embroidering Our Heritage.)*

2) Consider your friends. Withdraw from the ones who are frightened by your pain, the ones who think there might have been something you could have done, should still do to change things, the ones who want to be "fair". Remember you have a right to judge and to be angry. Don't forget Hecate. When you're hurting, you need especially considerate tenderness. As lonely as you may feel, it's better to have fewer or no friends than those who won't care to understand. Perhaps it is fear of friends' lack of sensitivity which sends so many women to therapists — to pay for a supposedly nonjudgmental caring with a hidden agenda of "fitting" into the therapists norms, whatever those may be.

3) Take charge of your sorrow. It will take some time to project ahead and think when the pain will be over,

but with effort, you'll be able to see that end. Pain comes in and out like waves. When it recedes, you may feel it is over. Then another wave engulfs you. That's when you must remember that there will be a time when it will be past — a time you can name. Not next week, not next month. Maybe in three months. Maybe not until Fall or Spring. Whenever it is, set it as a goal. Know you can survive until then. Meanwhile, take the time between to make an ending ritual. Jews burn a candle for eight days after a loved one dies. The candle is in a tall glass, and as the flame burns lower the upper part of the glass darkens until the flame goes out by itself and the glass is all dark. Other candles are lit on the anniversary of the death, and on particular holidays.

Create a ritual. Remember — a ritual has symbolic meaning — so whatever you choose to do must have significance for you. And a ritual must be repetitive. You must be able to do it again and again — times when you don't seem to need it, and times when you can't imagine that it will help. For example — a candle can be marked off in days and burned, a little each day. Maybe pictures or letters should be burned, or, if you prefer, torn in small pieces and sent off in running water — a little each day or week, until the bad time is past. Sometimes anger requires a hex. Remember, Z Budapest has said a witch that cannot hex cannot heal.

4) Remember the healing power of work, if it is work you love and in which you believe. Remember a feminist is a woman who recognizes the common oppression of women and will struggle against it. We need to imagine repairing, reweaving, mending the damage done, as Mary Daly points out, and then to do it.

HOW TO BE A GRIEVERS FRIEND

A griever's friend is one who is there, who spends more time than seems reasonable with a griever. She listens and understands. She isn't Polyanna. She's angry at her friend's pain. She values loyalty over fairness. She doesn't say "You should have" or "Why didn't you" or "Now you should", and she tries not to let the griever think that way about herself. She tells the griever over and over that what has happened is not fair, not deserved; that anger is justified.

214

A NOTE ON DYING

Maybe it is not until our own death becomes imminent,
palpable, that we can consider how we live. Those of us
who have been told we have some fatal disease are
faced with choices about our living, now. Of course, we
all know someday we will die, yet we don't know it until
we are told the day is near, is set. Then the remainder of
living is thrown into sharp focus, whether it is daily
behavior or what we let the doctors do to delay the
event. Certainly the one in four women with breast
cancer must face this reality. Those of us who have
spent time with someone dying, when it is not taken
entirely from our hands by the medical profession, and
when it is not sudden and/or violent, know that it is a
transformation that possesses its own wonder, triumph,
and joy.

(See *The Cancer Journals* and "A Litany for Survival"
in *The Black Unicorn* by Audre Lorde; *Green Paradise
Lost* by Elizabeth Dodson Gray; and *Dreaming the
Dark* by Starhawk.)

BIBLIOGRAPHY

Also see the bibliography in *The Political Palate*, since we have not duplicated entries. This applies to all sections.

FAVORITE COOKING RESOURCES

Jaffrey, Madhur, *World of the East Vegetarian Cooking*. New York, NY: Alfred A. Knopf; 1981.

Antreassian, Alice, and Jebejian, Mariam, *Classic Armenian Recipes: Cooking Without Meat*. New York, NY: Ashod Press; 138-40 64th Ave., Flushing, 11367; 1981.

Withim, Gloria, *Elegant Eating in Hard Times*. Trumansburg, NY: Crossing Press; 1983.

Manners, Ruth Ann and William, *The Quick & Easy Vegetarian Cookbook*. New York, NY: M. Evans and Co., 1978.

Nearing, Helen, *Simple Food for the Good Life*. New York, NY: Delacorte; 1980.

Canter, David and Kay, and Swann, Daphne, *The Crank's Recipe Book*. Oxford, England: J.M. Dent and Sons, Ltd.; 1982.

Warrington, Janet, *Sweet and Natural*. Trumansburg, NY: Crossing Press; 1982.

Colbin, Annemarie, *The Book of Whole Meals*. Brookline, MA: Autumn Press; 25 Dwight Street, 02146; 1979.

Kushi, Aveline Tomoko, *How to Cook with Miso*. Elmsford, NY: Japan Publishing; 200 Clearbrook Road, 10523; 1978.

Greene, Diana Scesny, *Sunrise: A Breakfast Cookbook*. Trumansburg, NY: Crossing Press; 1980

Geiskopf, Susan, *Putting it up with Honey*. Ashland, OR: Quicksilver Productions; P.O. Box 340, 97520; 1979.

Avery, Jane and Rob, *Making Your Own Preserves*. Dorchester, Dorset, England: Prism Press; Stable Court, DT2 OHB; 1981

Kraft, Ken and Pat, *Exotic Vegetables*. New York, NY: Walker and Co.; 720 Fifth Avenue, 10019; 1977

Lincoff, Gary, *The Audubon Society Field Guide to North American Mushrooms*. New York, NY: Knopf/Borzoi; 1981

Russell, Helen Ross, *Foraging for Dinner*. Nashville, TN: Thomas Nelson Inc.; 1975

Richardson, Joan, *Wild Edible Plants of New England.* Yarmouth, ME: Delorme Publ. Co.; 1981.

Brackett, Babette, and Lash, Maryann, *The Wild Gourmet: A Forager's Cookbook.* Boston, MA: David R. Godine;1975 1975

Carson, Dale, *Native New England Cooking.* Old Saybrook, CT: Peregrine Press; 1980

Sharpe, Ed, and Underwood, Thomas, *American Indian Cooking & Herb Lore.* Cherokee, NC: Cherokee Publ.; P.O. Box 124; 1973.

Turner, Nancy, J., *Food Plants of British Columbia Indians: Part I — Coastal Peoples.* Victoria, British Columbia: B.C. Provincial Museum; 1975.

Groff, Betty, and Wilson, Jose, *Good Earth Country & Cooking.* Harrisburg, PA: Stackpole Books; Cameron and Kelker Streets, 17105; 1974

―――――, *Country Goodness Cookbook.* Garden City, NY: Doubleday; 1981.

Uvezian, Sonia, *Cooking from the Caucasus.* New York, NY: Harcourt, Brace, Jovanich; 1976.

Siegel, F., *Russian Cooking.* Chicago, IL: Imported Publ.; 320 W. Ohio Street, IL 60610; 1974.

Bolotnikova, V.A. et al, *Byelorussian Cuisine.* Chicago, IL: Imported Publ.; 320 W. Ohio Street, IL 60610; 1979.

Georgievsky, N.J. et al, *Ukranian Cuisine.* Chicago, IL: Imported Publ.; 320 W. Ohio Street, IL 60610; 1975.

Roden, Claudia, *A Book of Middle Eastern Food.* New York, NY: Random House; 1974.

Machlin, Edda Servi, *The Classic Cuisine of the Italian Jews.* New York, NY: Everest House; 1981

Calingaert, Efrem Funghi, and Serwer, Jacquelyn Days, *Pasta and Rice Italian Style.* New York, NY: Charles Scribner's Sons; 1983.

Singh, Manju Shivraj, *The Spice Box: Vegetarian Indian Cookbook.* Trumansburg, NY: Crossing Press; 1981.

Sacharoff, Shanta Nimbark, *Flavors of India.* San Francisco, CA: 101 Productions; 834 Mission Street, CA 94103; 1972.

Sahni, Julie, *Classic Indian Cooking.* New York, NY: William Morrow; 1980.

Dandekar, Varsha, *Salads of India.* Trumansburg, NY: Crossing Press; 1983.

Tsuji, Shizuo, *Japanese Cooking: A Simple Art.* New York, NY: Kodansha International; 1980.

Ortiz, Elizabeth Lambert, *The Complete Book of Japanese Cooking.* New York, NY: M. Evans Co., 1976.

Solomon, Charmaine, *The Complete Asian Cookbook*. New York, NY: McGraw-Hill; 1976.

Brennan, Jennifer, *The Original Thai Cookbook*. New York, NY: Putnam/Perigee; 1981.

Ok, Cho Joong, *Home Style Korean Cooking in Pictures*. New York, NY: Kodansha; 1981.

Bayley, Monica, and Le Foll, Alain, *Black Africa Cook Book*. San Francisco, CA: Determened Productions, Inc.; P.O. Box 2150, CA 94126; 1977.

Burt, Elinor, *Spanish Dishes from the Old Clay Pot*. Berkeley, CA: Ross Books; P.O. Box 4340, 94704.

Ortiz, Elizabeth Lambert, *The Book of Latin American Cooking*. New York, NY: Random House; 1979.

A FEMINIST BIBLIOGRAPHY

FOOD FOR THOUGHT: A SUBJECTIVE LIST

GENERAL

Daly, Mary, *Pure Lust*. Boston, MA: Beacon Press; 1984.

Dworkin, Andrea, *Right Wing Women*. New York, NY: Putnam-Perigee; 1983.

_____, *Pornography: Men Possessing Women*. New York, NY: Putnam; 1979.

Griffin, Susan, *Pornography and Silence*. New York, NY: Harper and Row; 1981.

Frye, Marilyn, *The Politics of Reality: Essays in Feminist Theory*. Trumansburg, NY: Crossing Press; 1983.

Moraga, Cherrie, and Anzaldúa, Gloria, *This Bridge Called My Back: Writings by Radical Women of Color*. New York, NY: Kitchen Table, Women of Color Press; P.O. Box 2753, Rockefeller Center Station, 11215; 1983.

Beck, Evelyn Torten, *Nice Jewish Girls*. Trumansburg, NY: Crossing Press; 1982.

Grahn, Judy, *Another Mother Tongue: Gay Words, Gay Worlds*. Boston, MA: Beacon Press; 1984.

Faderman, Lillian, *Surpassing the Love of Men*. New York, NY: William Morrow; 1981.

Rush, Florence, *The Best Kept Secret*. New York, NY: McGraw-Hill; 1981.

Linden, Robin; Pagano, Darlene; Russell, Diana; and Leigh Star,
    Susan, *Against Sadomasochism: A Radical Feminist Analysis*. East
    Palo Alto, CA: Frog In The Well; 430 Oakdale Road, 94303; 1982.

Smith, Barbara, *Home Girls*. New York, NY: Kitchen Table, Women
    of Color Press; 1983.

Gomez, Alma, and Moraga, Cherrie, *Cuentos: Stories by Latinas*.
    New York, NY: Kitchen Table, Women of Color Press; 1983.

Lorde, Audre, *Sister Outsider*. Trumansburg, NY: Crossing Press;
    1984.

_____, *Uses of the Erotic: The Erotic as Power*. New York, NY:
    Out and Out Books; 476 Second Street, Brooklyn, NY 11215; 1978.

Rich, Adrienne, *Compulsory Heterosexuality and Lesbian Existence*.
    Denver CO: Antelope Publications; 1612 St. Paul, 80206; 1980.

Brant, Beth, *A Gathering of Spirit, Sinister Wisdom #22-23*. Rockland,
    ME: P.O. Box 1023, 04841; 1983.

Cochran, Jo; Escudero, Bettina; et al, *Bearing Witness:
    Sobreviviendo*. Corvallis, OR: Calyx: P.O. Box B, 97339; 1984.

Spender, Dale, *Women of Ideas and What Men Have Done To
    Them*. Boston, MA: Ark Paperbacks; 1982.

Russ, Joanna, *How to Suppress Women's Writing*. Austin, TX:
    University of Austin Press; 1983.

Giddings, Paula, *When and Where I Enter . . . The Impact of Black
    Women on Race and Sex*. New York, NY: William Morrow; 1984.

Schoenfielder, Lisa, and Weiser, Barb, *Shadow on a Tightrope*. Iowa
    City, IA: Aunt Lute Book Company; P.O. Box 2723, 52244; 1983.

Chernin, Kim, *The Obsession: Reflections on The Tyranny of
    Slenderness*. New York, NY: Harper and Row; 1981.

Delacoste, Frederique, and Newman, Felice, *Fight Back!: Feminist
    Resistance To Male Violence*. Minneapolis, MN: Cleis Press, P.O.
    Box 8281, 55408; 1981.

Johnson, Sonia, *From Housewife to Heretic*. Garden City, NY:
    Doubleday/Anchor; 1983.

McNaron, Toni, and Morgan, Yarrow, *Voices In The Night: Women
    Speaking About Incest*. Minneapolis, MN: Cleis Press; 1982.

Caldicott, Helen, *Missile Envy*. New York, NY: William Morrow;
    1984.

McAllister, Pam, *Reweaving The Web Of Life*. Philadelphia, PA:
    New Society Publishers; 4722 Baltimore Avenue, 19143; 1982.

Meyerding, Jane, *We Are All Part of One Another*. Philadelphia, PA:
    New Society Publ.; 1984.

Cook, Alice, and Kirk, Gwyn, *Greenham Women Everywhere*.
    Boston, MA: South End Press; 302 Columbus Avenue, 02116;
    1983.

Allport, Catherine, *We Are the Web*. New York, NY: Artemis Project; 156 Sullivan Street, 10012; 1984.

Parham, Barbara, *What's Wrong With Eating Meat?* Denver, CO: Ananda Marga Publ.; 854 Pearl Street, 80203; 1979.

Mason, Jim, and Singer, Peter, *Animal Factories*. New York, NY: Crown Publishers, Paperback; 1984.

Barry, Kathleen, *Female Sexual Slavery*. New York, NY: Avon; 1979.

_____, Bunch, Charlotte, and Castley, Shirley, *International Feminism: Networking Against Female Sexual Slavery*. New York, NY: International Women's Tribune Center, 777 U.N. Plaza, 10017; 1984.

Solanas, Valerie, *Scum Manifesto*. London, England: Matriarchy Study Group, 190 Uppper Street; 1983.

Steinem, Gloria, *Outrageous Acts and Everyday Rebellions*. New York, NY: Holt, Rinehart; 1984.

Nicarthy, Ginny, *Getting Free: A Handbook For Women In Abusive Relationships*. Seattle: Seal Press; 312 S. Washington, 98104; 1982.

Fuentes, Annette, and Ehrenreich, Barbara, *Women in the Global Factory*. Boston, MA: South End Press; 1983.

Ehrenreich, Barbara, *The Hearts of Men*. Garden City, NY: Doubleday/Anchor; 1984.

Jones, Ann, *Women Who Kill*. New York, NY: Fawcett Columbine Books; 1980.

Walker, Alice, *In Search of Our Mother's Gardens*. New York, NY: Harcourt, Brace, Jovanovich; 1984.

Sterling, Dorothy, *We Are Your Sisters*. New York, NY: W.W. Norton; 1984.

Cornwell, Anita, *Black Lesbian in White America*. Tallahassee, FL: Naiad Press, P.O. Box 10543, 32302; 1983.

Hull, Gloria T.; Scott, Patricia Bell; and Smith, Barbara, *But Some of Us Are Brave*. Old Westbury, NY: The Feminist Press, Box 334, 11568; 1982.

Joseph, Gloria, and Lewis, Jill, *Common Differences: Conflicts in Black and White Feminist Perspectives*. Garden City, NY: Doublday/Anchor; 1981.

Moraga, Cherrié, *Loving in the War Years*. Boston, MA: South End Press, 302 Columbus Avenue, 02116; 1983.

Randall, Margaret, *Sandino's Daughters*. Vancouver, B.C., Canada: New Star Books; 2504 York Avenue, V6K 1E3; 1981.

Jordan, June, *Civil Wars*. Boston, MA: Beacon Press; 1981.

Chicago, Judy, *Embroidering Our Heritage*. New York, NY: Doubleday; 1981.

Hammond, Harmony, *Wrappings*. New York, NY: Mussman Bruce Publ.; 139 West 22nd Street, 10011; 1984.

Lippard, Lucy, *Overlay*. New York, NY: Pantheon Books; 1983.

Whitechapel Art Gallery, *Frida Kahlo and Tina Modotti*. London, England; 1982.

Hayden, Dolores, *Redesigning the American Dream*. New York, NY: W.W. Norton; 1984.

Oda, Mayumi, *Goddesses*. Berkeley, CA: Lancaster-Miller Publ., 3165 Adeline St., 94703; 1981.

Endicott, Marion, *Emily Carr*. Toronto, Ontario, Canada: Women's Educational Press, 280 Bloor Street W., Ste 313, M5S IW1; 1981.

Leghorn, Lisa, and Parker, Katherine, *Woman's Worth*. Boston, MA: Routledge and Kegan Paul; 1981.

Oakley, Ann, *Subject Woman*. New York, NY: Pantheon Books; 1981.

Schwarz, Judith, *Radical Feminists of Heterodoxy*. Lebanon, NH: New Victoria Publ., 7 Bank Street, 03766; 1982.

Senesh, Hannah, *Her Life and Diary*. New York, NY: Schocken Books; 1971.

Taylor, Barbara, *Eve and the New Jerusalem*. New York, NY: Pantheon Books; 1983.

Snitow, Ann; Stansell, Christine; and Thompson, Sharon, *Powers of Desire*. New York, NY: Monthly Review Press; 1983. (Introduction is valuable history)

Keller, Evelyn Fox, *A Feeling for the Organism: The Life & Work of Barbara McClintock*. New York, NY: W.H. Freeman and Co.; 1983.

Chernin, Kim, *In My Mother's House*. New York, NY: Harper and Row; 1983.

Simon, Kate, *Bronx Primitive*. New York, NY: Harper and Row; 1983.

Sayre, Anne, *Roasalind Franklin and the DNA*. New York, NY: W.W. Norton and Co.; 1975.

Sarton, May, *Plant Dreaming Deep*. New York, NY: W.W. Norton; 1968.

Martin, Wendy, *An American Tryptich*. North Carolina: University of North Carolina Press; 1984.

Bernikow, Louise, *Among Women*. New York, NY: Harper and Row; 1980.

Mander, Jerry, *Four Arguments for the Elimination of Television*. New York, NY: William Morrow; 1977.

Chesler, Phyllis, *About Men*. New York, NY: Bantam; 1978.

Mamonova, Tatyana, *Women and Russia.* Boston, MA: Beacon Press; 1984.

Swallow, Jean, *Out From Under: Sober Dykes and Our Friends.* San Francisco, CA: Spinsters Ink, 803 De Haro Street, 94107; 1983.

Fairchild, Betty, and Hayward, Nancy, *Now That You Know: What Every Parent Should Know About Homosexuality.* New York, NY: Harcourt Brace; 1979.

Roberts, J.R., *Black Lesbians.* Tallahassee, FL: Naiad Press; 1981.

Chapkis, W., *Loaded Questions: Women in the Military.* Washington, DC: Institute For Policy Studies; 1981.

Beneke, Timothy, *Men on Rape.* New York, NY: St. Martin's Press; 1982.

Clifford, Denis, and Curry, Hayden, *A Legal Guide for Lesbian and Gay Couples.* Berkeley, CA: Nolo Press; 950 Parker Street, 94710; 1980.

Obbo, Christine, *African Women: Their Struggle for Economic Independence.* London, England: Zed Press; 1981.

El Dareer, Asma, *Woman, Why Do You Weep?.* London, England: Zed Press; 1982.

Tawil, Raymanda Hawa, *My Home, My Prison.* New York, NY: Holt, Rinehart, & Winston; 1979.

El Sadawi, Nawal, *The Hidden Face of Eve: Women in the Arab World.* Boston, MA: Beacon Press; 1980.

Adnan, Etel, *Sitt Marie Rose.* Sausalito, CA: Post-Apollo Press; 35 Marie Street, 94965; 1982.

Gray, Elizabeth Dodson, *Patriarchy as a Conceptual Trap.* Wellesley, MA: Roundtable Press, 4 Linden Square, 02181; 1982.

_____, *Green Paradise Lost.* Wellesley, MA: Roundtable Press; 1979.

Gilligan, Carol, *In a Different Voice.* Cambridge, MA: Harvard University Press; 1982.

Pogrebin, Letty Cottin, *Growing Up Free.* New York, NY: Bantam; 1980.

Luker, Kristin, *Abortion and the Politics of Motherhood.* Los Angeles, CA: University of California Press; 1984.

Arcana, Judith, *Our Mothers' Daughters.* Berkeley, CA: Shameless Hussy Press; P.,O. Box 3092; 1979.

Federation of Feminist Women's Health Centers, *A New View of a Woman's Body.* New York, NY: Simon & Shuster; 1981.

_____, *How to Stay Out of the Gynecologist's Office.* Culver City, CA: Peace Press; 1981.

Cassidy-Brinn, Ginny; Hornstein, Francie; and Downer, Carol, *Woman Centered Pregnancy and Birth*. Minneapolis, MN: Cleis Press; 1984.

Cohen, Nancy, and Estner, Lois, *Silent Knife: Caesarian Prevention*. South Hadley, MA: Bergin and Harvey Publ.: 670 Amherst Road, 01075; 1983.

Chesler, Phyllis, *With Child: A Diary of Motherhood*. New York, NY: Berkeley; 1980.

McCauley, Carole Spearin, *Surviving Breast Cancer*. New York, NY: E.P. Dutton; 1979.

Lorde, Audre, *The Cancer Journals*. San Francisco, CA: Spinsters Ink; 803 De Haro Street, 94107; 1980.

McDonald, Barbara, with Rich, Cynthia, *Look Me In The Eye: Old Women, Ageing & Ageism*. San Francisco, CA: Spinsters Ink; 1983.

Mestel, Sherry, *Earth Rites Vol. I, Herbal Remedies*. New York, NY: Earth Rites Press; 398 8th Street, Brooklyn, NY, 11215; 1978.

Spignesi, Angelyn, *Starving Women*. Dallas, TX: Spring Publ., P.O. Box 222069, 75222; 1983.

Campling, Jo, *Images of Ourselves*. Boston, MA: Routledge and Kegan Paul; 1981.

Matthews, Gwyneth Ferguson, *Voices from the Shadows*. Toronto, Ontario, Canada: Women's Educational Press; 1983.

Duffy, Yvonne, . . . *All Things Are Possible*. Ann Arbor, MI: A.J. Garvin Assoc.; P.O. Box 7526, 48107; 1981.

Bloch, Alice, *Lifetime Guarantee*. Watertown, MA: Persephone Press; 1981.

Leunig, Mary, *There's No Place Like Home*. New York, NY: Penguin; 1982.

Sims, Margot, *On The Necessity of Bestializing the Human Female*. Boston, MA: South End Press; 1982.

Smith, Abbe, *Carried Away: The Chronicles of a Feminist Cartoonist*. Bridgeport, CT: Sanguinaria, 85 Ferris Street, 06605; 1984.

Hollander, Nicole, *"Mercy, it's the revolution and I'm in my bathrobe"*. New York, NY: St. Martin's Press; 1982.

————, *"My weight is always perfect for my height — which varies"*. New York, NY: St. Martin's Press; 1982.

————, *"Hi, this is Sylvia"*. New York, NY: St. Martin's Press; 1983.

Clinton, Kate, *Making Light*. Cazenovia, NY: Whyscrack Records; P.O. Box 93, 13035; 1982.

————, *Making Waves*, Cazenovia, NY: Whyscrack Records; 1984.

Hart, Nett, and Lanning, Lee, *Dreaming*. Minneapolis, MN: Word Weavers; P.O. Box 8742, 55408; 1983.

_____, *Ripening*. Minneapolis, MN: Word Weavers; P.O. Box 8742, 55408; 1983.

Turtle Grandmother Books, P.O. Box 33964, Detroit, MI 48232. A resource for materials on Native American and Women of Color Books.

National Women's Mailing List, 1195 Valencia Street, San Francisco, CA 94110. To get mailings of interest to feminists, organized by interest categories.

FICTION

Lorde, Audre, *Zami: A New Spelling of My Name*. Trumansburg, NY: Crossing Press; 1984.

Wilson, Barbara, *Walking on the Moon*. Seattle, WA: The Seal Press; P.O. Box 13, 98111; 1983.

Walker, Alice, *The Color Purple*. New York, NY: Wakshington Square Press; 1982.

Azpadu, Dodici, *Saturday Night in the Prime of Life*. Iowa City, IA: Aunt Lute Books, P.O. Box 2568, 52244; 1983.

Bloch, Alice, *The Law of Return*. Boston, MA: Alyson Publ., 40 Plympyon Street, 02118; 1983.

Wittig, Monique and Zeig, Sande, *Lesbian Peoples: Material For A Dictionary*. New York, NY: Avon; 1979.

Rule, Jane, *Outlander*. Tallahassee, FL: Naiad Press; P.O. Box 10543, 32302; 1982.

Robinson, Marilynne, *Housekeeping*. New York, NY: Bantam; 1980.

Piercy, Marge, *Braided Lives*. New York, NY: Ballantine; 1982.

Straayer, Arny Christine, *Hurtin' and Healin' and Talkin' It Over*. Chicago, IL: Metis Press; 1980.

Morgan, Claire, *The Price of Salt*. Tallahassee, FL: Naiad Press; 1984.

Blais, Marie-Claire, *Nights in the Underground*. Toronto, Ontario, Canada: General Publ.; 1982.

Brady, Maureen, *Folly*. Trumansburg, NY: Crossing Press; 1982.

Mohin, Lilian, and Shulman, Sheila, *The Reach and Other Stories*. London, England: Onlywomen Press, 38 Mount Pleasant, WCIX AP; 1984.

Lynch, Lee, *Old Dyke Tales*. Tallahassee, FL: Naiad Press; 1984.

Covina, Gina, *The City of Hermits*. Berkeley, CA: Barn Owl Books; 1101 Keeler Avenue, 94708; 1983.

Geller, Ruth, *Pictures from the Past.* Buffalo, NY: Imp Press; P.O. Box 93, 14213; 1978.

Wilson, Barbara, *Ambitious Women.* San Francisco, CA: Spinsters Ink, 803 De Haro Street, 94107; 1982.

Silko, Leslie Marmon, *Ceremony.* New York, NY: New American Library; 1977.

Cliff, Michelle, *Abeng.* Trumansburg, NY: The Crossing Press; 1984.

Thomas, Joyce Carol, *Marked by Fire.* New York, NY: Avon; 1982

Hubert, Cam, *Dreamspeaker.* New York, NY: Avon; 1978.

Bulkin, Elly, *Lesbian Fiction.* Watertown, MA: Persephone Press; 1981. Available from Gay Presses of New York, P.O. Box 294, Village Station, New York, NY 10014

Walker, Alice, *The Third Life of Grange Copeland.* New York, NY: Harcourt, Brace, Jovanovich; 1970.

_____, *In Love and Trouble.* New York, NY: Harcourt, Brace, Jovanovich; 1967.

_____, *You Cant Keep A Good Woman Down.* New York, NY: Harcourt, Brace, Jovanovich; 1971.

_____, *Meridian.* New York, NY: Pocket Books; 1976.

Emecheta, Buchi, *The Joys of Motherhood.* New York, NY: George Braziller; 1979.

_____, *The Slave Girl.* New York, NY: George Braziller; 1977.

Head, Bessie, *The Collector of Treasures.* London, England: Heinemann; 1977.

Kogawa, Joy, *Obason.* Boston, MA: David R. Godine; 1981.

Laurence, Margaret, *The Stone Angel.* New York, NY: Bantam; 1964.

_____, *The Diviners.* New York, NY: Bantam; 1982.

Smyth, Donna, *Quilt.* Toronto, Ontario, Canada: The Women's Press; 16 Baldwin Street; 1982.

Ozick, Cynthia, *Levitation.* New York, NY: E.P. Dutton; 1983.

Greenberg, Joanne, *High Crimes and Misdemeanors.* New York, NY: Holt, Rinehart & Winston; 1979.

Miner, Valerie, *Blood Sisters: An Examination of Conscience.* New York, NY: St. Martin's Press; 1982.

Rule, Jane, *Against the Season.* Tallahassee, FL: Naiad Press; 1984.

_____, *Contract with the World.* Tallahassee, FL: Naiad Press; 1982.

Hurston, Zora Neale, *I Love Myself When I Am Laughing.* Old Westbury, NY: The Feminist Press; P.O. Box 334, 11568; 1979.

Meigs, Mary, *The Medusa Head.* Vancouver, B.C., Canada: Talonbooks; 201 1019 E. Cordova, V6A 1M8; 1983.

_____, *Lily Briscoe: A Self Portrait*. Vancouver, B.C., Canada: Talonbooks; 201 1019 E. Cordova, V6A 1M8; 1981.

McCunn, Ruthanne Lum, *A Thousand Pieces of Gold*. San Francisco, CA: Design Enterprises; P.O. Box 14695, 94114; 1981.

Ballantyne, Sheila, *Imaginary Crimes*. New York, NY: Penguin; 1982.

Godden, Rumer, *An Episode of Sparrows*. New York, NY: Harper and Row; 1955.

Pym, Barbara, *Excellent Women*. New York, NY: Harper and Row; 1978.

Tyler, Anne, *Dinner at the Homesick Restaurant*. New York, NY: Alfred A. Knopf; 1982.

Tax, Meredith, *Rivington Street*. New York, NY: William Morrow; 1982.

Allen, Paula Gunn, *The Woman Who Owned the Shadows*. San Francisco, CA: Spinsters Ink; 803 De Haro Street, 94107; 1983.

Birtha Becky, *For Nights Like This One*. East Palo Alto, CA: Frog In The Well, 430 Oakdale Road, 94303; 1983.

Marshall, Paule, *Brown Girl, Brownstones*. Old Westbury, NY: The Feminist Press; Box 334, 11568; 1981.

Gordimer, Nadine, *July's People*. New York, NY: Penguin; 1983.

Bryant, Dorothy, *Ella Price's Journal*. Berkeley, CA: Ata Books, 1928 Stuart Street, 94703; 1972.

_____, *Killing Wonder*. Berkeley, CA: Ata Books, 1928 Stuart Street, 94703; 1981.

_____, *A Day in San Francisco*. Berkeley, CA: Ata Books, 1928 Stuart Street, 94703; 1982.

Grae, Camarin, *The Winged Dancer*. Chicago, IL: Blazon Books; 1934 W. Belle Plaine, 60613; 1983.

Shockley, Ann, *Say Jesus and Come to Me*. New York, NY: Avon; 1981.

McConnell, Vicki, *Mrs. Porter's Letter*. Tallahassee, FL: Naiad Press; 1982.

Ramstetter, Victoria, *The Marquise and the Novice*. Tallahassee, FL: Naiad Press; 1983.

Taylor, Valerie, *Prism*. Tallahassee, FL: Naiad Press; 1982.

Bannon, Ann, *I Am A Woman*. Tallahassee FL: Naiad Press, Volute Books; 1959.

_____, *Odd Girl Out*. Tallahassee FL: Naiad Press, Volute Books; 1957.

_____, *Beebo Brinker*. Tallahassee FL: Naiad Press, Volute Books; 1962.

Olivia, *Olivia*. London, England: The Hogarth Press, Ltd.; 1949.

Fleming, Kathleen, *Lovers in the Present Afternoon.* Tallahassee, FL: Naiad Press; 1984.

Manning, Rosemary, *Open The Door.* London, England: Jonathan Cape Ltd.; 1983.

SCIENCE FICTION/FANTASY

Hall, Sandi, *The Godmothers.* London, England: The Womens Press; 1982.

Llywelyn, Morgan, *The Horse Goddess.* New York, NY: Pocket Books; 1982.

Tiptree, Jr., James (Alice Sheldon), *Out of the Everywhere.* New York, NY: Ballantine; 1981.

Vinge, Joan, *The Snow Queen.* New York, NY: Dial Press; 1980.

Bradley, Marion Zimmer, *The Mists of Avalon.* New York, NY: Random House; 1982.

Russ, Joanna, *Extraordinary People.* New York, NY: St. Martin's Press; 1984.

Berseniak, Louky, *The Euguelionne.* Victoria, BC: Press Porcepic, 217-620 View Street, V8W 1J6; 1976.

Adam, Helen, *Ghosts and Grinning Shadows.* Brooklyn, NY: Hanging Loose Press; 231 Wyckoff, 11217; 1979.

McKillip, Patricia, *The Forgotten Beasts of Eld.* New York, NY: Avon; 1974.

Karr, Phyllis Ann, *Frostflower and Thorn.* New York, NY: Berkeley; 1980.

————, *Frostflower and Windborn.* New York, NY: Berkeley; 1982.

WOMANSPIRIT

Cameron, Anne, *Daughters of Copperwoman.* Vancouvr, B.C., Canada: Press Gang, 603 Powell Street; 1981.

Walker, Barbara, *The Women's Encyclopedia of Myths and Secrets.* San Francisco, CA: Harper and Row; 1983.

Brindle, June Rachuy, *Ariadne.* New York, NY: St. Martin's Press; 1980.

Starhawk, *Dreaming The Dark: Magic Sex and Politics.* Boston, MA: Beacon Press; 1982.

Monaghan, Patricia, *The Book of Goddesses and Heroines.* New York, NY: E.P. Dutton; 1981.

Stone, Merlin, *Ancient Mirrors of Womanhood.* Boston, MA: Beacon Press; 1984.

Noble, Vicki, *Motherpeace Tarot.* New York, NY: Harper and Row; 1983.

Heschel, Susannah, *On Being a Jewish Feminist*. New York, NY: Schocken Books; 1983.

Heresies, *The Great Goddess*. New York, NY: Heresies; 225 Lafayette Street, 10012; 1982.

Spretnak, Charlene, *The Politics of Women's Spirituality*. Garden City, NY: Doubleday; 1982.

Mazow, Julia Wolf, *The Woman Who Lost Her Names*. San Francisco, CA: Harper and Row; 1980.

Schneider, Susan Weidman, *Jewish and Female*. New York, NY: Simon & Schuster; 1984.

POETRY

Bulkin, Elly, and Larkin, Joan, *Lesbian Poetry*. Watertown, MA: Persephone Press; 1981. Available from Gay Presses of New York, P.O. Box 294, Village Station, New York, NY 10014.

Rich, Adrienne, *Sources*. Woodside, CA: The Heyeck Press; 25 Patrol Court, 94062; 1983.

_____, *A Wild Patience Has Taken Me This Far*. New York, NY: W.W. Norton; 1981.

Klepfisz, Irena, *Keeper of Accounts*. Sinister Wisdom (See periodical bibliography); 1982

Lorde, Audre, *Chosen Poems — Old And New*. New York, NY: W.W. Norton; 1982.

Teish, Luisah, *What Dont Kill Is Fattening*. San Francisco, CA: Fantree Press; 2861 McBryde Avenue, Richmond, CA 94804.

Allison, Dorothy, *The Women Who Hate Me*. Brooklyn, NY: Long Haul Press; Box 592, Van Brunt Station, NY 11215; 1983.

Clark, Cheryl, *Narratives*. New York, NY: Kitchen Table Press, P.O. Box 2753, Rockefeller Center Station, 11215; 1982.

Rukeyser, Muriel, *The Collected Poems of Muriel Rukeyser*. New York, NY: McGraw-Hill.

Piercy, Marge, *The Moon Is Always Female*. New York, NY: Alfred A. Knopf; 1982.

_____, *The Twelve Spoked Wheel Flashing*. New York, NY: Alfred A. Knopf; 1981.

_____, *Circles On The Water*. New York, NY: Alfred A. Knopf; 1981.

_____, *Stone, Paper, Knife*. New York, NY: Alfred A. Knopf; 1983.

Oriethyia, *Love Song to the Warriors*. Setauket, NY: Lenachild Press; 21 Detmer Road East, 11733; 1977.

Pacosz, Christina, *Notes From the Red Zone*. Seattle WA: Seal Press; Box 13, 98111; 1983.

Harjo, Joy, *What Moon Drove Me To This?*. New York, NY: J. Reed
Books; 285 E. Third Street, 10019.

Kaye, Melanie, *We Speak in Code*. Pittsburgh, PA: Motheroot Publ.;
214 Dewey Street, 15218; 1980.

Bruchac, Joseph, *Songs from This Earth on Turtle's Back*. Greenfield
Center, NY: The Greenfield Review Press; 1983.

Hacker, Marilyn, *Taking Notice*. New York, NY: Alfred A. Knopf; 1980.

Chambers, Jane, *Warrior at Rest*. New York, NY: J.H. Press, P.O.
Box 294, 10014; 1984.

Cruikshank, Margaret, *New Lesbian Writing*. San Francisco, CA:
Grey Fox Press; 1984.

Tsui, Kitty, *The Words of a Woman Who Breathes Fire*. San
Francisco, CA: Spinsters, Ink, 233 Dolores #8, 94103; 1983

CHILDREN

Fitzhugh, Louise, *Nobody's Family is Going to Change*. New York,
NY: Dell; 1974.

Garden, Nancy, *Annie on My Mind*. New York, NY: Farrar Straus
and Giroux; 1982.

Severence, Jane, *Lots of Mommies*. Chapel Hill, NC: Lollipop
Power; P.O. Box 1171, 27514; 1984.

Homan, Dianne, *In Christina's Toolbox*. Chapel Hill, NC: Lollipop
Power; P.O. Box 1171, 27514; 1982.

Gardner-Loulan, JoAnn, *Period*. San Francisco, CA: Volcano Press;
330 Ellis Street, 94102; 1979.

Yarbrough, Camille, *Cornrows*. New York, NY: Coward-McCann; 1979.

Caines, Jeannette, *Just Us Women*. New York, NY: Harper and
Row; 1982.

Dayee, Frances *Private Zone*. Edmonds, WA: The Charles Franklin
Press; 18409 90th Avenue West, 90820; 1982.

Meyer, Linda, *Safety Zone*. Edmonds, WA: The Charles Franklin
Press; 18409 90th Avenue West, 90820; 1984.

Colao, Flora, *Your Children Should Know*. New York, NY: Bobbs
Merrill; 1984.

Waxman, Stephanie, *Growing Up Feeling Good*. Los Angeles, CA:
Panjandrum Books; 1979.

Bell, Ruth, *Changing Bodies, Changing Lives*. New York, NY:
Random House; 1980

Scoppetone, Sandra, *Happy Endings Are All Alike*. New York, NY:
Dell.

Hamilton, Virginia, *Sweet Whispers Brother Rush*. New York, NY:
Avon; 1982.

Blank, Joni, *A Kid's First Book About Sex*. Burlingame, CA: Yes Press; P.O. Box 2086, 94010; 1983.

Council On Interracial Books For Children, *Homophobia Bulletin*. New York, NY: 1841 Broadway, 10023; 1983.

PERIODICALS

The Blatant Image. 2000 King Mountain Trail, Sunny Valley, OR 97497.

Calyx. P.O. Box B, Corvallis, OR 97339.

Common Lives. Lesbian Lives. P.O. Box 1553, Iowa City, 52244.

Conditions. P.O. Box 56, Van Brunt Station, Brooklyn, NY.

Lilith. 250 West 57th Street, New York, NY 10019

Fireweed. P.O. Box 279, Station B, Toronto, Canada M5T 2W2

Ikon. P.O. Box 1355, Stuyvesant Station, New York, NY 10009

Lesbian Contradiction. 1007 North 47th, Seattle, WA 98103 or 584 Castro Street, Suite 263, San Francisco, CA 94114

Lesbian Inciter. P.O. Box 7038, Powderhorn Station, Minneapolis, MN 55407

New Directions for Women. 223 Old Hook Road, Westwood, NJ 07675.

New Women's Times. 804 Meigs Street, Rochester, NY 14620

Maize. Word Weavers, Box 8742, Minneapolis, MN 55408

Off Our Backs. 1724 20th Street NW, Washington, DC 20009

Plexus. 545 Athol Avenue, Oakland, CA 94606

Sinister Wisdom. P. O. Box 1023, Rockland, ME 04841

Trivia. P.O. Box 606, North Amherst, MA 01059

Womanews. P.O. Box 220, Village Station, New York, NY 10014

Women of Power. P.O. Box 827, Cambridge, MA 02238

Women's Review of Books. Wellesley College, Wellesley, MA 02238

MUSIC

York, Beth, *Transformations*. Calliope Music; 519 South Candler Road, Decatur, GA 30030; 1983.

Wetzler, Laura, *Touch and Go*. Listen To This Productions; P.O. Box 499, Centerport, NY 11721.

Millington, June, *Running*. Fabulous Records; Emeryville, CA; 1983.

————, *Heartsong*. Fabulous Records; Emeryville, CA; 1981.

Troia, Lenore and Grier, *Gut Reaction*. Synergy Records; New Haven, CT; 1983.

Ferron, *Shadows on a Dime*. Penknife Productions, Lucy Records;
P.O. Box 67, Saturna Island, Vancouver, B.C., Canada VON 2YO.

Winter, Cathy, and Rose, Betsy, *Strong Singers*. Origami Enterprises;
Framingham, MA; 1982.

Near, Holly, *Speed of Light*. Redwood Records; P.O. Box 996, Ukiah,
CA 95482; 1983.

_____, *Watch Out*. Redwood Records; 1984.

_____, *Fire in the Rain*.Redwood Records; 1981.

Gardner, Kay, *Moods and Rituals*. Even Keel Records; 1981.

_____, *A Rainbow Path*. Ladyslipper; P.O. Box 3124 Durham, NC
27705; 1984.
Ladyslipper is a good source for women's tapes and records.

Culver, Casse, *Songs and Other Dreams*. Sweet Alliance Music; 1982.

Christian, Meg, and Williamson, Cris, *Meg/Chris at Carnegie Hall*.
Second Wave Records, Olivia; 1983.

Aspen, Kristin, and MacAuslay, Janna, *Musica Femina*. Musica
Femina; 1984.

Marciano, Rosario, *Piano Works by Women Composers*. Moss Music
Group; 1979.

Casselberry and DuPree, *Caselberry and DePree*. She Lion
Productions; 1983.

Bishop, Heather, *I Love Women*. Mother of Pearl; Woodmere,
Manitoba, RO 1 2MO Canada; 1982.

Mama Quilla, *Mama Quilla*. Tupperwaros Records; 1982.

Alive!, *City Life*. Alive! Records; 1000 Nevarro Bluff Road, Albion, CA
95410; 1984.

_____, *Call it Jazz*. Redwood Records; 1981.

Scneewittchen, *Zerschlag deinen glassernen sarg*. Phonogram Gm
bH; West Germany; 1978.

Cox, Ida, *Wild Women Don't Get the Blues*. Rosetta Records; 115
West 16th Street, New York, NY 10011.
Other jazz women's records available from the same source:

Snow, Valaida, *Hot Snow*.

White, Georgia, *Georgia White Sings and Plays the Blues*. Rosetta
Records.

Reagan, Judy, *Old Friends*. Wild Patience Records; P.O. Box 6330,
Arlington, VA 22206; 1983.

Reagan, Toshi, *Demonstrations*. Cassette, 1984.

INDEX